SOUNDBITES FROM HEAVEN

*What God Wants Us to Hear When
We Talk to Our Kids*

RACHAEL CARMAN

Published by Focus on the Family, Colorado Springs, CO 80995.

Focus on the Family and the accompanying logo and design are federally registered trademarks of Focus on the Family, Colorado Springs, CO 80995.

Library of Congress Cataloging-in-Publication Data
Carman, Rachael, 1966-
      Soundbites from heaven : what God wants us to hear when we talk to our kids / Rachael Carman. — 1st ed.
         p. cm.
      ISBN-10: 1-58997-312-7
      ISBN-13: 978-1-58997-312-1
      Parents—Religious life. 2. Parent and child—Religious aspects—Christianity. Parenting—Religious aspects—Christianity.
I. Title.
            BV4529.C425 2005
            242'.645—dc22

      2005008013

Printed in the United States of America

CONTENTS

To my children: Charles, Anderson, Savannah Anne,
Molly, Elizabeth, Joseph, and Benjamin,
who have taught me so much about myself and my God.
You are each such a unique blessing to me.
I am looking forward to talking, listening,
and learning much more with each of you!

———

To my readers, and everyone who wants to hear
from our heavenly Father.

ACKNOWLEDGMENTS

This part is the real challenge. So many people have contributed in so many ways to this book. I'm grateful that this list is so long!

First I'd like to thank those who encouraged me to write before it was even on my radar screen. Thank you to Bev Tucker and Carol Hicks, along with many conference and retreat attendees who were the first to plant this idea in my mind.

Next I want to thank the RDC Ministries prayer team: Debbie Hobel, Janette Cancellieri, Jamie Vanderveer, and Faye McBroom. I also want to thank the other prayer warriors who carried me through this project, specifically Mary George, Sarah Baptista, Jan Porter, Carolyn Husk, Sue McConnell, and Lisa Edwards.

Thank you to the Proverbs 31 Ministry and She Speaks, through which I learned how to put a book proposal together. At their conferences I was given the opportunity to meet and present my proposals to potential publishers. Lysa TerKeurst, Rene Swope, Ginger Plowman, and Marie Ogram were great sources of information, encouragement, and prayer.

A special thanks goes to the Real Refreshment Retreat leadership team 2004 as it supported and prayed me through this writing project. The following graciously filled in many gaps and extended me patience as I tried to multitask: Carol Lynn Simons, Cheri Friesz, Dinki Sumural, Laura Silver, Jackie Elliot, Mindy Winters, Kathy Tousignant, Ruth Komer, and Karen Sydnor.

Thank you to Mark Maddox, who caught my passion and vision for the book and shared it with others at Focus on the Family. I will never forget the voice message from his assistant, Les Shaw, saying Focus was interested in publishing my "next book." Did I miss something? This is my first book!

The Focus team has been awesome, making me feel like part of the family. John Duckworth, my editor, has patiently answered my e-mails and given much insight and direction as I struggled to find my voice. Mary Sloan kept in touch through e-mails, birthday cards, and flowers while we were moving. Thank you also to Nanci McAlister, who was helpful and encouraging, keeping me informed of details and deadlines. Lance Roth and Brent Klassen also worked diligently to make the book a success.

Kim Thomasson provided regular words of encouragement, moments of levity, and passionate prayer on my behalf. She is the sister I never had, but have always longed for. Everyone should have a friend as dedicated, honest, loyal, gracious, and kind as she is. I love you, girl!

Thanks to my earthly father, Jerry McCaghren, who taught me about a gracious heavenly Father and placed within my heart a desire to listen to Him and follow Him only. And to my mother, Nancy McCaghren, whose words of wisdom still ring in my ears and serve me well today.

Thanks to my beloved husband, Davis, who never doubted, always prayed, and was always there to listen, read, and re-read all of my writings. His support and sacrifices throughout this project have been such a blessing to me!

DEAR READER

Hey, there!

So why did you pick up this book? I would love to know.

Did you just have some time to kill at the bookstore? Maybe you were bored, but your spouse was perusing the new titles and your kids were watching a video. In an effort to be considerate, you patiently walked around. Then you noticed this book; it sounded interesting, so you picked it up.

Maybe the idea that God might have something to say to you drew you in. Part of you really wants to believe there's a God, and that He cares.

Or could it be that you're a Christian—but can't imagine God would want to speak to you personally? You may think of Him as silent, just looking down and going about His business far away. You've heard others talk about a deep and abiding personal relationship with Him, but it's remained impersonal for you.

Someone out there is picking up the book because that "God as your Father" thing isn't working. You had a lousy earthly father; if he was any indication of how your heavenly Father feels about you, you've heard it all before. The parental sayings in this book may be foreign to you. "Shut up!" "Go away!" or "You'll never amount to anything" were the things you heard.

You won't find those in the table of contents. Those sayings would make the list for a book entitled, *The Things Earthly Fathers Say That Our Heavenly Father Would Never Say.*

Still another reason you might have picked up this book: You're blue in the face from trying to get your kids to listen to you. You talk, sermonize, lecture, and talk some more, but they just stare. Your heart is breaking and you're beyond the end of your rope. You see other parents, and their kids actually seem to listen to them. How do they do it?

Whatever the reason, welcome to my life!

In the following pages you'll read stories from our everyday adventures as a family with seven children. Some of the stories are funny and some are serious, but all are true. I've also reflected on my childhood experiences and daily struggles.

I welcome you to see someone who isn't perfect (though I've sometimes wanted to be), someone who's seeking to be perfected through Christ's perfect love. I believe some of the situations you'll read about will make you smile. I trust you'll relate to these realities and recognize yourself in many of them.

More than anything else, I hope that reading these anecdotes will make you want to listen to Him. Hearing from Him is awesome; His inspired Word, His glorious creation, and the promptings of the Holy Spirit have much truth to show and tell you personally.

The Creator of the Universe has something He wants to say! Are the ears of your heart prepared to listen? He made you with glorious plans in mind, and longs to have an intimate and unique relationship with you.

My prayer—and I've been praying for you as I've written every word—is that you'll start, if you haven't already, to hear His voice. He's not a tyrant, dictator, or sheriff. He's the Master of the universe, the King of kings, the Great I Am, the Holy One.

He's also your heavenly Father. That makes you His child.

He loves you. You're the apple of His eye. Your ultimate purpose is to glorify Him in all you say and do. His will is that you have a growing relationship as you seek Him, listen to His voice, and follow Him.

Writing this book has been an amazing journey. The stories I've shared are personal and make me feel vulnerable. I've been honest about my failures and weaknesses. My goal has been to create in you a yearning to listen to Him, and a readiness to act on what you hear.

Don't miss the introduction! In it I tell the story of the day when this paradigm shift first occurred for me. It started the idea for the book you're reading.

May you enjoy reading my stories and listening to His voice!

INTRODUCTION

I don't know what I thought I was getting myself into when I started having kids over 14 years ago. But I know this is not it.

Like most young, green parents, I was idealistic. I was looking forward to raising my kids so they wouldn't misbehave like other people's children. I even enjoyed dressing them and was an obsessive neat freak.

I knew all the horror stories, the ones everyone (even perfect strangers) tells you when you're pregnant. I knew there would be difficult days filled with spit-up, tantrums, whining, misplaced poop, sleepless nights, high fevers, and night terrors. In some ways I was prepared for all that.

But I wasn't prepared for what I faced one average day.

Like most mothers, I'd gotten into a daily pattern of using phrases to keep the crew in line. You've probably used some:

"How many times do I have to tell you to make your bed?"

"Stop hitting your brother!"

"Go to time out."

I worked hard to throw in "I love you!" when I thought about it, too.

On this particular day, one of my children was being passively disobedient. My response was a sermonette composed of frequently heard phrases: "What part of this is foggy to you? Do you understand what I am trying to tell you to do? What is the problem? I will not ask you to do something that I do not believe you are able to do, or which I am unwilling to help you with. Are you even listening to me?"

Suddenly time froze. It was as if I could hear God talking to me: "Yeah, Rachael, are *you* listening to *Me*? I think I have been pretty clear. I have some things I would like for you to do, and I promise to help you. Let's work together."

My own chided child had disappeared during this moment of revelation. I was left to contemplate my heavenly Father's questions.

I was convicted. I hadn't been listening. I'd been hearing, but not obeying. I'd been passively disobeying, the very sin I'd been quick to point out to my child—but was ignoring in myself.

On that fateful day I discovered that the kids and I are in this together. I saw that the very things God is trying to root out in my character providentially show up in my children.

I'd become accustomed to my sin, not even calling it that; it was "just who I am." But upon spotting it in my kids, I was appalled and became determined to obliterate it.

That moment became a turning point in my perspective as a parent. From that day on, everything I said to my kids took on new meaning and became an opportunity for introspection.

I've been overwhelmed with the connection between what I say to my kids and what God is trying to say to me. Sometimes I can almost hear His voice: "Be still. I am God, that's why. Please trust and obey Me. Where have you been? Pay attention. Take the trash out." Now, when I talk to my kids about their behavior, attitudes, and responsibilities, my heart is more in tune with what God is saying to me.

I pray that this little book will change your perspective, too—that it will cause you to remember that you're still a child, His child. As your heavenly Father, He wants to communicate His feelings, concerns, questions, wisdom, and encouragement to you. More than anything else, He loves you. He wants an ongoing relationship with you.

Before you read the rest of this book, though, I'd like to give you a challenge. List the top 10 things you hear yourself say most often to your kids. Then ask your kids to list the top 10 things they hear you say most frequently. If you're brave, you could even ask the same question of other people.

The resulting lists will give you a starting place to explore the things God wants *you* to hear.

Then enjoy reading these stories. Let them remind you of times when you heard your parents say similar things to you. But most importantly, listen for His voice.

"He who has ears to hear, let him hear" (Mark 4:9).

SPEAKING OF SPEAKING

Throughout this book I write about hearing from God. I don't mean this in the literal sense of hearing an audible voice. I mean that I have a strong, clear, undeniable awareness of His will for me. I use words like "whisper," "said," "prods," "insists," "replies," "asks," and "speaks" as I describe "hearing" from Him.

In the Old Testament God audibly spoke to Adam, Noah, Abraham, Samuel, and others. I believe that if He wanted to speak to me in that way, He would. But the way He does speak to me, through His written Word, in my heart, is still very intimate. The kind of communication I'm talking about requires me to listen with the ears of my heart.

He is the Good Shepherd, and He proclaims that His sheep know His voice (John 10:3-5).

> "I remember
> the day you
> were born."

I have seven great stories about the births of my kids.

Charles came first, a forced labor. I remember thinking I'd never have another baby. I discovered firsthand all the things no one tells you about childbirth, and it wasn't pretty!

Two years later Anderson arrived, quite larger than his older brother. They nearly had to take him by C-section, but the mention of it motivated me to almost shoot him across the room.

The day that our first daughter appeared, it was snowing in Charlotte, North Carolina. Upon her arrival Savannah Anne smiled.

Molly actually came on her due date. And she came really fast—in only three pushes.

For number five, I was induced again. Elizabeth came into the world. She's been a gentle spirit from the beginning.

I almost walked a trench around the nurses' station trying to get Joseph's debut going, but to no avail. He took his time and arrived five hours later. I was exhausted!

Little Benjamin's big day was delightfully uneventful and peaceful after a very busy nine months of pregnancy.

These are probably my kids' favorite stories to hear, followed closely by how my husband, Davis, and I met. They love to hear how I counted their fingers and toes, how I kissed them, and how they cried. They also love to look at their baby pictures.

They ask all kinds of questions: "Did I have hair?" "When did I smile?" "Who did I look like?"

I love to tell these stories. And I love to hear *my* mother tell about *my* arrival—how her water broke, causing the doctor to fall in the hall! There's something about hearing your birth recounted that makes you feel special.

God remembers your grand entrance, too. He's known you from the dawn of creation, chose the time of your birth, and understands the circumstances. Like a new father who holds his child for the first time, He had plans for you.

He wants you to know that He knows. Whether the situation surrounding your birth was positive or negative, He cares. His plan is to work in and through you either way.

God knows everything about you. He knows the number of hairs on your head.

"I remember the day you were born," He says.

I remember another special day, too. It was a cool spring morning. My five-year-old son, Anderson, and I were sitting in our car outside the place where the kids took music lessons. Suddenly Anderson announced, "Mom, I want to have Jesus in my heart."

"Come here, Anderson," I said. He got out of his car seat

and made his way into my lap. We were cramped, but cozy. "What do you mean?" I asked.

"I want to be a Christian," he said. "They were talking about it at church. They said that Jesus wants to be my best Friend."

"That's right, Anderson, He does," I said. As he sat in my lap, we prayed.

I'll always remember that day, when Anderson was born . . . again.

If you've accepted Christ as your Savior, your heavenly Father remembers that day, too. He recalls the moment you were born again into His new life, the moment you chose Him.

He remembers the commitment you made to follow and trust Him, how childlike your faith was, how innocent you were about the challenges you'd face. He remembers everything about that special day.

It's great that He remembers, but it's important that we remember, too. We need to think back on the day we were reborn into His family. We need to recall where we came from and what He did for us when He cleaned us up. It will help to keep us humble, if we let it.

It's important to admit how much we needed Him then and how much we need Him now. We need to remember the promises we made when we came into the family, too. Did we promise to follow no matter where, no matter what? Did we promise to trust all alone in the dark?

"I remember the day you were born," He says.

And He asks: "Do you?"

A Moment of Introspection

- If you're a parent, what are the stories of your children's birthdays?
- What are your—and their—favorite parts of the stories?
- Have you been "born again"? If so, what were the circumstances? If not, please see the "Becoming a Child of God" section at the end of this book for information on taking this important step of faith.

> ## "Do you know where you're going?"

I don't remember my Dad using a map when I was growing up. That's not to say he always knew *how* to get where he was going, but he always knew where he was headed.

Many times I got into the car with him and asked, "Well, where are we going?"

"To so-and-so in Dallas," he would answer confidently.

Then I would inquire, "Do you know how to get there?"

"No," he would answer, "not really. But we will get there." And we always did. There may have been a shorter route, or one with less traffic, but we managed to arrive all the same.

"Do you know where you're going?" Asking me this question might be pointless, since I'm directionally challenged. If we're lost and I say, "I think we should go left," by all means, turn right. If I say, "I think we've passed it," it's probably still ahead. And if I say, "I think I know where I am," be afraid—be very afraid.

I ask this question of my kids, of course. When the boys head out the door with their soccer ball I ask, "Where are you going?"

To them it seems obvious: "Outside."

I ask them to be more definitive. "Where outside?"

"Just out front to play ball," they reply.

"Okay, have fun! And stay close by in case I need you!"

"Yes, Ma'am!"

Later in the afternoon the girls want to go "outside," too.

"Where are you going?" I ask.

"Down to the neighbor's house to play," they answer.

It seems easy enough to them; it's just three houses down. But as a mom, I know a lot can happen between our house and that of their friends. I agree, then call my neighbor Cheri when the girls have gone. I watch them from the window as they make the short trek. They know where they're going; I just want to make sure they make it.

So, do you know where you're going? Not just on Friday night, or on your errands, or on vacation—but eternally?

The answer matters because it will affect where you go and what you do today.

I know where I'm going, but sometimes I take a wrong turn. I find myself way down the road, far off course—all because I stopped listening to God, forgot where I was headed, and insisted on taking over the wheel.

He doesn't wrestle the wheel back from me. He waits for me to turn it back over to Him.

Here's good news: No matter where you are, you *can* get where He wants you to be. It's all about listening to the Navigator.

Where we go matters. We aren't called to wander around aimlessly. We're to run the race set before us, wherever He leads us.

We'll face deserts, valleys, mountaintops, canyons, and crossroads. To reach our destination—becoming like Him—we'll have to keep our eyes fixed on Him, determined to go wherever He leads.

Many people think they know where they're going. They even believe they're making progress in getting there. But they're following the wrong map. To reach the destination God has for you, you have to follow His map.

Do you know where you're going?

And will the path you take today get you closer to that destination—or further away?

A Moment of Introspection

- If you have kids, do you ask where they're going when they leave your home? If so, why? How do they respond?
- Do you know where you're going? Why or why not?
- How do your plans for today relate to your ultimate destination? What can you do during the next 24 hours to get you one step toward the goal of becoming more like Jesus?

"Slow down!"

Do you have one? I do.
I *am* one.

By that I mean a person who usually operates in fifth gear. But we'll get to me in a minute.

It's a typical morning in the Carman household; we're all working, going, trying to get breakfast on the table. Elizabeth is getting napkins, Molly spoons and vitamins. Savannah Anne mixes Benjamin's rice cereal. Anderson finds Joseph's bib and cup while Charles pours water for hot chocolate. Joseph is the only idle one, sitting and munching on "yo-yos"—his name for Cheerios.

Once we're at the table, cereal and milk are passed and poured. Then it happens.

In the same way that it happens every morning across America as families have breakfast, the milk gets spilled—in slow motion. A hush falls over the crowd—the other children. Every one tenses and looks to Mom. How will she respond?

Will it be . . .

A. "Oops!"

B. "Can you just pour the milk in a glass?"

C. "Please slow down!"?

The milk drips off the table as I choose C.

"But I wasn't going too fast," the culprit replies, getting towels to sop up the mess. He doesn't see that his speed has anything to do with the spilt milk. To him they're independent issues. I can see they're clearly related.

Why do I really want him to slow down? Because he's been rushing all morning. Before he spilled the milk, there were warning signs. He bumped into his sister, ignored his little brother, and was rude to Elizabeth. Spilling the milk finally stopped him and got his attention, but it wasn't the first indication he was going too fast.

Oh, I can relate to this one! I get going on a project or thought and want everyone to catch up with me. I focus so totally on getting something done that I think of people as roadblocks.

"Slow down," I can almost hear God say as I'm racing along.

"I can't!" I reply. "I have a deadline. People are depending on me. I have to get this done."

When that happens, God sends people to get my attention like flashing lights on a racetrack. A friend calls to say "Hi." I get an e-mail from someone who needs direction. Elizabeth wants to paint. Anderson finds an interesting bug. Benjamin needs to nurse.

Will I slow down so that I can serve and enjoy those around me? Will I trust the One who holds all time to help me meet my deadline, or will I insist on handling it myself? Am I going to stop for the red light or run it?

In my experience, there's far more to be gained through interruptions—pit stops, detours, and side roads—than there is to be lost. I gain a smile, a breath of fresh air, a new perspective, a glimpse of His glory when I pause at the intersection and look around.

I notice this when I help Elizabeth get set up to paint, and when I sit down with her to create pictures, too. That's when I build our relationship. I learn who she is and what she likes. As she rambles on about her masterpiece, I enjoy her company and look forward to the years to come. Over the long haul, those moments matter.

Without those moments—times when I've slowed down to be with her—I can't expect her to slow down for me. I suspect that someday I'll want that. I'll want her to spend her valuable time on me, to look at my paintings, to listen to me ramble.

God wants me to slow down so that He can show me Himself. He wants me to see the sunrise like watercolors in the sky, the rainbow in the fall leaves as they reflect the sun's first rays, the wings of honking geese as they fly overhead, the crisp coolness of the morning with frost sparkling on the leaves.

When I race ahead, uninterested in slowing down, determined to do what needs to be done, I allow the urgent to eclipse His majesty.

When I slow down, I am confronted with the undeniable truth: He is an awesome God, Maker of heaven and earth! The heavens declare His glory (Psalm 19).

God doesn't want me to wait until I see the flashing red lights of a pursuing police car to slow down. Chances are that, like the spilt milk, it would not be the first indication that I was going too fast.

Oh, the peace available to all of us—if we would just slow down.

A Moment of Introspection

- If you have children, when do they tend to go too fast?
- Have you talked to them about the value of down-shifting? How have you modeled this for them? What activities help you slow down and relax together?
- What gear do you typically function in? If you're going too fast, why do you suppose that is? What part of God's creation could you enjoy more today if you just slowed down?

4

> ## "It's time
> ## to get up!"

"Good morning to you,
Good morning to you;
It's time to get up,
The sky is all blue!"

"The time has come to rise and shine,
To rise and shine,
To rise and shine;
The time has come to rise and shine
So early in the morning!"

"This is the day (this is the day)
That the Lord has made (that the Lord has made);
I will rejoice (I will rejoice)
And be glad in it (and be glad in it)!"

"Get up!
Get up for Jesus, you sleepy heads.
Get up!"

These are the types of songs my kids are likely to hear first thing in the morning. My mother started the tradition in an effort to avoid the fuss and fighting usually associated with getting kids out of bed.

She would cheerfully enter the room, singing as she opened the curtains. "Time to get up!" she would announce. My mom, a combo of Lucille Ball and Carol Burnett, could be really cheesy. But I have fond memories of her singing before dawn's early light.

Unfortunately for Mom, I was not then nor am I now a morning person. I enjoy the morning—the sunrise, the dew, the newness of it all—after I'm up. But getting upright is sometimes the hardest thing I do all day.

I remember a Ziggy cartoon from many years ago in which he said, "I would like morning much better if it came later in the day." Me, too.

It seems to be hereditary. When I go into my children's rooms in the morning and announce, "It's time to get up!" I am not usually met with eagerness to start the day. No matter what song I choose, they wish they could sleep a little longer.

They try all the usual techniques: ignoring, complaining, arguing, feigning illness. "Do we have to?" they ask. They roll over, snuggle under the covers, put pillows over their heads. They hope my call is part of a bad dream.

But just like dear ol' Mom, I persist. I sing another stanza. I make up a cheesy song on the fly.

"That doesn't even rhyme, Mom," they mutter. Or sometimes the verdict is, "Hey, Mom, not too bad."

Either way, the song is followed by, "It's time to get up! God has a great day planned for us. So let's get going!"

They start waking and moving. They yawn and rub their eyes—and we're off!

What my kids don't know is that my mornings start much as theirs do. I hear the alarm and try to ignore it.

Then I seem to hear God saying, "Rachael, it's time to get up! I have so much planned for you today. I have some things I need to prepare you for. It's time to get up so that we can spend some time together getting ready for the day ahead."

"Can we just do it here, while I doze? I am *so* tired. Could we maybe do it later? Pleeeasse?" And I roll over, hoping to get just a few more minutes of rest.

"It's time to get up!" He persists. "Trust Me. I will meet your every need today. I know that you didn't get much sleep last night, but if you will get up and spend time with Me, I will sustain you through this day beyond what you could ask or imagine."

Having wasted 15 minutes arguing and rolling over and over, I usually get up at this point—knowing He has proven Himself faithful so many times and anticipating what He will reveal to me today as I seek Him first. But there are still days when I ignore the invitation to fellowship from the King of kings and sleep on.

I believe God wants the first part of our day. He wants us to put Him first in everything. He wants us while we're still fresh.

He wants to prepare us for the day ahead, to set our focus. He wants us to meditate on His goodness, to get up and spend time with Him early because He knows how difficult it will be later.

When Christ was on earth, there were times when He went out to pray early in the morning, while it was still dark. He's our example. I believe His will for us is to "seek first his kingdom and his righteousness, and all these things will be given to you as well" (Matthew 6:33).

God wants to bless us in a myriad of ways. It all starts with our heeding His early morning call: "It's time to get up!"

A Moment of Introspection

- If you have kids, how do you wake them in the morning?
- What's the first thing you do in the morning?
- Do you ever spend time with God after you get up? If so, how does it tend to affect your day? If not, how do you think it could?

5

> ## "That is not how we treat our brothers and sisters."

Perhaps there's an audiotape available of this quote. If so, you can put it on repeat play at our home. If your family is anything like mine, you find yourself saying this several times a day.

"We do not kick each other."

"We do not spit at each other."

"We do not speak rudely to each other."

"We do not . . . [fill in the blank]."

My husband and I are trying to teach our children that they're blessed to have brothers and sisters. We believe God has orchestrated our family with its different and similar personalities to bless one another and bring glory to His name.

So when the kids aren't showing brotherly affection toward one another, I say, "God did not send you these brothers and sisters to be a bother, but a blessing. You need to treat them like the blessing they are, and trust that God knows what He's doing."

It breaks my heart when I see my children hurt each other. Playing too rough, saying hurtful words, being stingy or selfish—they're all such ugly behaviors.

Take riding in the car, for example.

Is getting to ride in the front seat of the car a big, stressful deal in your family? It is in ours.

We've tried to come up with a simple method of determining whose turn is next. Once someone proposed keeping a log of who rode in the front seat, to where, and for what length of time. Ideally, rotations would occur every 30 minutes or 30 miles, whichever came first.

Now think about that. Is it really workable? With all the things I have to do, all the papers I already have to chase, all the time I need to account for, this seemed silly.

My solution: "When the issue arises, just do what you wish the other person would do."

"You mean give him the front seat?" my oldest asked.

"Is that what you wish he would do for you?"

"But," the kids responded in unison, "then I will never get to sit in the front seat!"

Man, they had missed the point.

I find that we adults have missed the point, too.

We've been blessed with brothers and sisters in the Lord, yet we talk to them with unkind words at times. We're rude or stingy. When that happens, God wants us to hear, "That's not how we treat our brothers and sisters."

As my kids tried to do with their siblings, we rewrite the Golden Rule to make it some kind of "even" exchange. We try to turn it into an "If you will, then I will" verbal contract with our brothers and sisters:

"I will share if you do."

"I will play your game now if we play my game next."

"I will forgive you if you forgive me."

"I will help you if you help me."

This gives us an escape clause, an excuse for our selfishness—the other person. If we didn't do what we were supposed to, it's because our brothers and sisters didn't do what they should have done.

A few years ago the letters "WWJD" (What Would Jesus Do?) were printed on everything from bumper stickers to wristbands to stationery. I heard a story about this that illustrates my point. A mother whose sons were arguing over the last piece of cake asked, "What do you think Jesus would do in this situation?"

The older son replied without hesitation, "Oh, Jesus would let the other person have the piece of cake."

The mother was proud of her son's response. But just as the other son reached for his treat, the older brother added, "Ben, why don't *you* be Jesus?"

Romans 12:10 says, "Be devoted to one another in brotherly love." That is how we treat our brothers and sisters.

Jesus said, "Greater love has no one than this, that he lay down his life for his friends" (John 15:13). That is how we treat our brothers and sisters.

We're to honor our spiritual siblings above our own needs and wants. We're to consider them first, choosing to serve them selflessly.

The Golden Rule isn't about being fair. It's about giving up our own way—willingly and cheerfully.

That is how we treat our brothers and sisters.

A Moment of Introspection

- If you're a parent, how are your children treating each other?
- How are you treating your brothers and sisters in the Lord? Are there some "toys" you need to share more freely? Are you satisfied with the way you talk about other believers? The church?
- How could focusing on Christ help you put others' needs before your own?

6

> *"Look at me."*

My kids and I get to share a lot of laughter—which bonds us in a unique way.

It happens when I say to one of the kids, "Look at me." That's because I proceed to accidentally call the kid I'm talking to by a sibling's name. I've been known to go through the whole list before I land on the name of the child who's standing before me.

The kids usually wait patiently for me to come to the right name. Sometimes they help me: "Mom, it's Elizabeth." Then she'll grin. She's looking at me, I'm looking at her—but her name escapes me. And I was the one who gave it to her!

One day while trying to cut Savannah Anne's hair, I really blew this saying. She kept turning her head, making it difficult for me to cut straight.

"Savannah Anne, keep your head still."

"Savannah Anne, stop moving your head."

"Savannah Anne, I'll be done in just a moment. Hold still."

Then I said it: *"Close your eyes and look at me!"*

She thought it was hysterical. She laughed and laughed, then called to her brothers and sisters, "Did you hear what Mom said this time? She said, 'Close your eyes and look at me.' Oh, Mom!"

Despite that mistake, there are good reasons for wanting my kids to look at me when I talk to them. I want to know I have their full attention. I want them to focus on what I'm saying. I want them to look into my eyes to see the love and commitment I have for them.

I need to see into their eyes, too. I need to see those eyes into which I've gazed so many times, going back over a thousand memories we've shared. These are the eyes I saw after they were born, so clear and blue, the eyes that were so wide open at all the wrong times those first few months in the middle of the night, the eyes in which I've learned to read love and fear and confusion and excitement, the eyes I've watched grow heavy at nap time and full of tears after a fall.

I also need to look into my kids' eyes to see if they're with me. This often happens when we're in Wally World (a.k.a. Wal-Mart) with all its distractions—TV monitors, other people, clothes, food, toys, pet supplies, screaming babies, and shopping carts.

When we are in Wally World, they aren't the only ones who are distracted. I often forget something a few aisles back and have to assign a pair of them to fetch the missed item. It's one of their favorite parts of a trip to the local grocer.

I've sent them back to aisle 7 for paper towels and they've returned with pretzels from aisle 4. I've sent them to aisle 2 for another gallon of milk and they've returned with cheese slices. What was I doing wrong? I didn't demand their attention.

Now I begin such grocery store commissions with this simple phrase: "Look at me." It's not a perfect system, but guess what? Since I've been having them "Look at me" before they head off on a mission, I've found that I'm more likely to get what I sent them for.

Of course there are times when they're looking at me and I wish they weren't. Those are the times when I'm acting ugly in my impatience or anger, or when I'm allowing my selfishness to take over like a monster. Those are the times when I'm focusing on me.

That's why I need to keep looking at *Him.* My job is to get them to seek *His* face, too—so that they won't be afraid to look to *Him* for everything.

But how can we "look at" an invisible God? In Hebrews we're told to fix our eyes on Jesus.

Look at His compassion, forgiveness, sacrifice, power, healing, and priorities. To "look at Him" means to imitate His example, walk in His footprints, take up our cross and follow Him.

When God urges us to look at Jesus, He's asking us to ignore distractions and gaze into the eyes that squinted at the brightness of the star upon His birth, that saw the woman at the well, that wept at the death of His friend, that spoke without words to His accusers. These are the eyes that saw us in the secret place when we were formed in our mother's womb, the eyes that see our hearts.

"Look at Me," He says. "This is what I want you to do. Seek Me, come to know Me. See in My eyes the love I have for you. Realize all the memories we share. Know that I have seen you from the beginning of time. Block the rest out and focus on Me. I have something significant to tell you. I love you; I have a plan for your life. Do you see who I am? I will take care of you. I will lead you through this.

"Look at Me."

A Moment of Introspection

- If you're a parent, when do you want your kids to look at you? When do you want them to *not* look at you?
- Have you ever tried to "turn your eyes upon Jesus"? If so, what happened?
- What do you think God sees when you look at Him?

7

"*You gave your word.*"

One morning I woke up in one of those moods. It continued unchecked, and I let myself get into a self-pity pit as the day wore on.

Since I like to clean my house to work through frustrations, I was feeling the need for a real house scrubbing. I like to do that alone, but this time it wasn't to be. My husband, Davis, was rushing out of the house to AWANA with the kids.

"Who are you taking?" I asked.

"Everyone but Benjamin and Charles—he'll help you!"

The door closed and Davis was gone. I needed to cry, but I didn't want to do it with Charles there. I felt stifled.

"So, Mom, what can I do to help you?"

Now *there's* a question every mom longs to hear. Charles could tell I was having a tough day, and his dad had charged him with being helpful. "Well," I said, "you can clean the kitchen."

"Okay," he said, and started working while I sat to nurse little Benjamin. I was tired and really appreciated the help. When Benjamin was done, I felt restless and decided to go into the backyard to see whether the zinnia seeds I'd planted had sprouted.

Charles, having cleaned the kitchen, joined me as I headed out the back door. "Is there any thing else I can do for you, Mom?" he asked.

"Well, yes. You can sweep up the pile in the kitchen corner, pick up the two spoons on the floor, and put away the dishes on the right side of the sink."

"Okay. Then do you think I could play outside?"

"Yes, it is a beautiful evening," I said. "It would be great for you to play outside. Thanks for all of your help. I love you."

"I love you, too, Mom!" he said as he hurried back inside.

The short walk to the garden had proved encouraging and invigorating. The tiny plants were on their way to providing us with a beautiful display of flowers to enjoy as we ate in our sunroom.

When I came back into the house, Benjamin was happily babbling to himself, bouncing in his saucer. Hearing the garage door close, I knew Charles was already enjoying the great outdoors.

Now I can get down to business, I thought. With the kitchen clean and swept, I could mop and vacuum.

That's when I saw it—the little pile in the corner that Charles had neglected.

I couldn't believe it. There was Charles in the backyard, playing with a friend. He was totally oblivious to his irresponsibility, footloose and fancy free, in his own world and having a great time.

He didn't see me when I said to him out loud, "You gave me your word."

Just as I said it to him, my Father seemed to whisper it to me: "Rachael, you gave Me your word, too."

Right then, the Holy Spirit starting bringing to mind all the things I'd promised my heavenly Father. Some I'd promised almost flippantly; others I'd solemnly vowed.

Charles had said he would sweep up a small pile of dust and Cheerios and Goldfish crumbs, and I'd depended on him to do it. Because he hadn't kept his word, I had to stop what I was doing and do his job.

Suddenly I was aware of all of the promises, all the times I'd given my word but hadn't followed through. All the times I'd forced on someone else the burden of doing my job because I didn't. All that wasted time, all those lost opportunities.

I realized that if I called Charles in to do what he'd said he would do, he'd have excuses like "I forgot," "I was going to," "I didn't mean to say I would," and "I thought it was optional." They were the same excuses I'd given my Father when He'd reminded me of vows I'd made.

I knew I'd lost out by being disobedient. After all, the Bible says it's better to not give your word and do something than to give your word to do something and not do it.

But someone else was missing out, too—the person who might be blaming God for not answering a prayer because I didn't follow through on meeting a need.

I could have called Charles back in that evening. I could have chided him. I could have made him not only sweep up the pile in the corner but also mop and vacuum.

But at that moment, the speck in his eye had nothing on the

log sticking out of mine. It was time for my Father and me to get down to business. God wanted to show me lovingly that all those things I'd promised were serious and mattered for His kingdom. They were not just little things.

He spoke to my heart as I mopped and vacuumed and cried.

Forgive me, Father, for not keeping my word, I prayed. *Give me Your strength to do better in the future.*

A Moment of Introspection

- If you're a parent, what have you taught your children about the importance of keeping their word?
- What excuses have they given you for not keeping promises? How have you responded?
- What are some issues on which you've given your word? Have you kept it? If you've let someone down, how could you rectify the situation this week?

8

> ## "How many times do I have to tell you?"

E ver since I realized that hitting the target was going to be a problem for the boys in the toilet training process, it's been their responsibility to clean up their missed shots—which are many.

It had originally been my hope that the grossness of this task would motivate them to aim better. I cannot, however, say that I have achieved my objective. In short, at 14 and 12 years of age, they are still primarily responsible for cleaning the toilet daily.

This has been their job for the better part of five years now. They're supposed to do it upon their first morning visit to the facilities. Not after breakfast, not after lunch, and not even after a reminder.

After all, it's been five years. How many times do I need to tell them?

They're able to remember when soccer practice starts, and where to find their favorite snacks. They never forget how to use their rollerblades. So what's the difference between the things I have to tell them over and over and the things they readily recall? The answer: the value they place on the information.

Soccer practice, snacks, and rollerblades are all important to the boys. Clean toilets are not.

I believe that in the long term, knowing how to clean a toilet and appreciate a clean toilet will benefit them. This will be the case even if they don't have to clean one regularly in the future. But they're unaware of the long term; they have yet to understand the value of personal hygiene, thoroughness, responsibility, and obedience. In the meantime, it is my job as mom to tell them over and over and over again.

Do you ever feel like a proverbial broken record in the things you say to your kids? Boy, I do.

Maybe you remember your parents saying certain things again and again to you, too. Maybe they replay in your mind. Some may have been painful and have had a damaging effect. Others may have sustained you throughout your life.

I'm trying to be more intentional instead of accidental with the things I say to my kids—especially the things I want them to remember. When I'm not around anymore, I want them to recall hearing me say, "I love you." So I say it in many different ways.

God is like that, too. There are many things in His Word that He says over and over with divine patience, without frustration, because He loves us. He had to repeat Himself for the same reasons I have to repeat myself as a mom.

Unfortunately, the main reason He has to repeat Himself is because I don't trust Him enough to take Him at His Word— or because I simply ignore Him. Still, He takes pleasure in reminding me daily that He loves me.

I believe there are five major statements that God says over and over throughout the Bible:

1. Love the Lord your God with all your heart, soul, mind, and strength.
2. Love your neighbor as yourself; love one another.
3. I love you.
4. Be strong and courageous; stand firm and live by faith.
5. I will never leave you nor forsake you.

When we doubt or question, when we rebel or give up, these are the things He wants us to hear Him saying. These are the messages that can revolutionize our lives when we embrace them. These are the cry of our God and Savior's heart. How many times does He have to tell us?

God wants you to hear His voice and accept His message. He wants you to let His grace and mercy wash over you, removing your sin, drawing you into a relationship with Him.

Hear the truth and grace in His Word as He whispers, "How many times do I have to tell you?"

A Moment of Introspection

- If you have children, what do you find yourself telling them over and over? Why do you do that?
- Are you repeating messages that will bless your children long after you're gone? What do you think they'll most remember you saying?
- What messages does God have to repeatedly send to you?

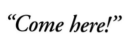

9

"Come here!"

Jonah. Here's a story we can all relate to. God has an assignment for Jonah to carry out, but Jonah doesn't want to do it. How many times has that happened to me?

When I was a kid, my mom would ask me to clean my room, do my homework, or wash the dishes. "I don't want to!" was my response.

But my mother in her wisdom would reply, "I did not ask if you wanted to. I am telling you to do it."

In a similar way, God said, "Jonah, I have a big job for you to do. I want you to go to Nineveh and preach a message of repentance to the people."

But Jonah replied, "I don't want to." In an effort to get out of the job, he booked himself on a ship going in the opposite direction. He went beyond "I don't want to" and added, "I won't."

Coming when you're called is hard for a lot of us—including my kids. When they don't respond to my voice, a little detective work usually tells me why.

In such cases, asking them where they've been is just a

formality. Let's see—dried mud on the edges of their shoes, a mud stripe down the middle of their backs, mud caked under their fingernails, fishy smell, purple mustaches. I'm thinking they went to the pond on their bikes through the mud, fished and caught turtles, and bought a Popsicle from the ice cream man. Busted.

It's not a bad thing for boys to hang out at the pond for the afternoon, if they have permission and come when I call them. But if their location keeps them from hearing my voice, we have a problem.

Sometimes when I call, they hear perfectly. But they want to know what's in it for them. If they respond to my voice, what do they get? A movie? A treat? A privilege? I want them to come because I called, not in search of a reward.

God is the same way with me. When He calls, He wants me to respond because of who He is, not for what He might give me. He calls in quiet moments, when I'm awed by a sunrise. He calls in the chaos of a busy day. He calls me at the crossroads of decision.

At sunrise He reminds me that He's the Creator God. In chaos, He tells me He's the Prince of Peace. At the crossroads, He extends His strength as I make a choice.

"Come here!" He calls. But too often I rush to the phone instead of the throne. Rather than going to the Bread of Life or the Living Water, I race to the world's empty well. Instead of talking it over with Him in prayer or seeking His will in His Word, I want to consult someone else.

"Come to me, all you who are weary and burdened, and I will give you rest," He says (Matthew 11:28). He wants me to draw near to Him, and promises to draw near to me. He wants me to sit straight up, anxious to hear His voice and act on what I hear.

"Come here" has an urgency about it. *Now* is implied; don't wait.

"Where have you been?" is a frustrated response to unanswered calls. "I needed you and you weren't here. You missed it. You forgot. How could you? I was depending on you.

"You can run, but you can't hide."

My kids know what I probably want them to do when I call them. That's why they sometimes ignore my beckoning. When they finally show up, the obvious question is, "Where have you been?"

I can usually tell where they've been. God can tell with us, too.

Yet the best place to hear from Him is wherever you are. He wants you to come from whatever you've been doing when He calls. He welcomes you into His light, and drives away the darkness with His love.

"Come here," He says. "Let Me see your face. Where have you been? I want you to know that I love you. You do not belong in that corner. I have a mansion prepared for you! Come with Me and let Me tell you all about it."

A Moment of Introspection

- If you have kids, when is it hardest to get them to respond to your call?

- Have you ever "drawn near" to God? If so, how? What happened?
- What tends to keep you from going to Him when He calls? If He asked, "Where have you been?" how would you answer?

"We don't act like that."

10

It has long fascinated me how royal families train their children from very young ages to act "properly." After all, they represent the crown; they are not mere commoners. No elbows on the table for them. No sticking out tongues, pointing fingers, or picking noses. Such behavior is inappropriate for royalty.

Many of us would love to know their secrets. How do you get a four-year-old to stop picking her nose in public? How do you get those elbows off the table? And please tell me the secret to getting my kids to stop pointing fingers.

I love to shop at Wal-Mart, which I affectionately refer to as Wally World. Not only can you buy almost anything there, you can see just about anything, too. It's a classroom in human behavior, a springboard for discussion.

One day we saw a truly remarkable, unforgettable drama play out in the checkout line. Two parents were purchasing a birthday gift for their toddler son to take to a party. The kid didn't care about the present; all he wanted was some M&Ms.

At first the parents' answer was no. They hadn't eaten lunch yet and were about to go to a party. But the child obviously knew the drill and persisted.

Finally they agreed to the purchase. But the tot wouldn't let the cashier have the candies to scan. The parents wrestled the package from him long enough to ring it up, then gave it back to calm him down—with the condition that he keep it closed until after lunch.

Shocker: Junior did not fall for this stipulation, either. He wanted the candies *now*.

A grabfest followed as the parents tried to gain control, which they'd apparently abdicated a while back. You guessed it—M&Ms went flying. It was a pretty ugly scene, and the worst was yet to come. The saddest moment arrived when the parents were actually on their hands and knees, picking up candy while the "winner" happily chomped down the rest.

When we got back to the car, my son commented on the scene: "Boy, Mom, you would never let us behave like that!"

I grew up a minister's daughter. From an early age I was taught that my every action, public or private, could have an impact on my father's ministry. But growing up in the proverbial fishbowl wasn't all bad. I learned to deny myself, to think before I acted, to consider others before myself. When I messed up, I felt embarrassed.

Now, with a family of our own, my husband and I have tried to instill in our children who they are and who they represent.

First and foremost, they represent Christ; they're Christians. They're sons and daughters of the King, heirs to the throne.

They have a crown and mansion awaiting them. We try to encourage them to behave accordingly.

Sometimes this can make it hard to fit in. But the Bible tells us Christians are strangers here, aliens (1 Peter 2:11-12). Fitting in isn't supposed to be our goal. Nonbelievers are to be drawn by our differences and want to know what we're all about. In turn, we're to be prepared to give an answer for the hope within us (1 Peter 3:15).

You and I are being watched every day. When we "don't act like that" it stands out. The world says hate those who hate you; as children of the King, we're to love those who hate us. The world says get, get, and then get some more; as children of the King, we're to give, give, and give some more.

In God's family, "We don't act like that." When that happens, the world will want to know, "What's up with that? Why are you being so nice, so patient, or so generous? How can you control yourself when situations around you are so out of control?"

The answer is, "Without Him, we can't. It's Christ in us, the hope of glory."

This is what it means to "Let your light shine before men, that they may see your good deeds and praise your Father in heaven" (Matthew 5:16). In God's family, we act in a way that brings glory to Him, not to ourselves.

As the saying goes, "Preach the gospel. Use words if you have to." People will want a relationship with Jesus when they see in us a people who spend time with Him and reflect Him in our actions.

"By this all men will know that you are my disciples, if you love one another" (John 13:35).

A Moment of Introspection

- Who do you represent? How do you think your everyday actions reflect on those you stand for?
- How would you act differently if your father were a king? Now that you know your heavenly Father is the King, how should you be acting?
- If you're a parent, how will you discuss with your children the things your family doesn't do? How about the things you *do*?

11

"*I love you!*"

These are words I took for granted growing up. I don't think a day went by without my mom and dad saying them to me. And that was just an echo of my heavenly Father's statement of the same.

They're also my favorite thing to say to my own kids. Nothing else gets a broader smile, a deeper sigh, a truer repentance.

"I love you!"

I like to say it in a variety of ways. I like to sing it to my children, whisper it—and yes, even yell it.

I like to say it when they least expect it—in the middle of a story we're reading together, or when they're biting their nails, or when we both know they're thinking about doing something they shouldn't. Sometimes I like to say it to them in my "You've really done it this time!" voice, which catches them off guard.

"I love you!"

I've found that these three words have incredible power. They can curb bad behavior, reel in rebellion, stop a step down a dangerous path, and draw kids back into the fold.

Sometimes it takes quite a bit of self-control on my part to

speak these three words instead of launching into one of my ser-
monettes. My speeches give me such pleasure and allow me to
let off steam, but at times all my kids really need is another "I
love you!"

On occasion I have to say these words to a child to remind
myself that I really do love him or her, even though I'm not feeling it at the moment. Loving really is a choice, a commitment.
The three little words have a tremendous calming affect on the
child and on me, affirming that our relationship is more important than anything. These words realign us opposite the problem, instead of allowing the problem to separate us.

The Bible teaches that "Love covers over a multitude of sins"
(1 Peter 4:8). When I see my children through the eyes of love,
there are many things I can overlook—like the fact that the towels they folded aren't perfectly straight, or that the table they were
to wipe still has sticky places. Love leaves room for improvement.

The whole gospel can be summed up in these three words.
God's message is, "I love you!"—boldface, underlined, exclama-
tion mark!

Just as this should be the number one thing you say to your
kids, it's the number one thing He wants you to hear from Him.
It motivates His pursuit of you and your heart. If you let it, it
will motivate your life choices. "I love you" is the center of it all.

That doesn't mean God doesn't discipline us. When a loving heavenly Father disciplines us, we may interpret it as unlov-
ing or unfair, but our perspective is wrong. None of my
children has ever asked to be vaccinated or take medicine, to be
limited in the number of sweets she can eat, or in how late he

can stay up at night. But setting and enforcing boundaries are an act of love on my part—often of the tough variety. So it is with God.

Throughout His Word, God is saying, "I love you." He patiently says it over and over in many different ways:

The Creation="I love you."

The Covenant="I love you."

The Ten Commandments="I love you."

Jesus Christ="I love you."

God knows that if we can ever get a handle on His love for us—not that we could ever understand its depth or length or height, but just accept that He loves us—it would profoundly and permanently change us. When you know someone loves you, it puts all that person's actions into perspective.

Listen for those three little words. In the breeze, in the warm sunshine, in the storm, in the busyness and in the stillness, listen and hear Him say it:

"I love you!"

A Moment of Introspection

- If you have kids, when was the last time you told them you love them? In what other ways do you communicate your love for them?
- Do you ever hear God saying, "I love you"? If so, how has He said it to you? How would you like Him to say it?
- When have you told God how much you love Him?

12

"Where is your brother?"

It was a rainy day. All the kids were tired and restless at the same time. It was Wednesday, our "nap day," when I usually can tackle a project or two.

But today no one was tired enough for a nap—just cranky. To the children's shock, I declared the afternoon "movie time." I even popped popcorn. Benjamin was the only one who went down for a nap; the others settled in to watch a video and munch on their treat.

"Look out for Joseph!" I said, referring to our two-year-old.

"Yes, Ma'am!" they answered.

I went into the other room to get started on my project. The kids were quiet except for occasional laughter.

Before I knew it, an hour had passed. I returned to the room where the kids were and took a head count. *Uh-oh, one short.*

"Where is your brother?" I asked, looking for Joseph. For a moment I was ignored in favor of *Toy Story*, but then I hit the PAUSE button on the remote.

"Where is your brother?" I asked again.

"I don't know," chorused the ones who weren't snoring.

"Well, we need to find him," I said.

Our search didn't take long. Joseph had found my stash of dark chocolate mini-pieces in the nightstand. Carefully unwrapping them, he'd lined them up on the floor to eat. He was about halfway down the line when we found him. It was hard not to laugh.

Although he was sneaking, Joseph was in no danger. But he could have been. I'd put him in his siblings' care, depending on them to keep up with him. Thankfully all he got into was chocolate!

"Where is your brother?" It's a simple question, but important. I want my kids to care enough to watch out for each other. I want them to have a growing relationship of love. I want them to protect each other.

Their relationships probably will outlast many other relationships in this life. They may not realize it, but other friendships may come and go; neighbors will come and go, and even their dad and I will go sometime. I want their relationships to weather the losses and celebrate the joys: their weddings, the births of their own children, and their ever-growing walk with Christ.

God wants me to have that kind of relationship with my brothers and sisters in Christ. When I'm hurting or celebrating He gently whispers, "Where is your brother or sister, Rachael? I've given you so many. There are so many to care, to lend a hand, to shed a tear, to lift up a prayer, to give a word of encouragement, to hold up your tired arms."

So where are my brothers and sisters in Christ? Some I've

neglected; some I've rejected. Some I've embraced; others I've used for my own selfish purposes. Others I've learned from, run from, grown with, or lost.

God has lovingly provided me with spiritual brothers and sisters so that I can experience His grace, forgiveness, love, joy, compassion, faithfulness, and patience. He knows how much I need them for the journey. He knows the value of their hugs and tears, laughter and silence, prayers and encouragement. He wants me to know where they are so that I can experience fellowship more completely.

We're all to be looking out for the interests of others. We're to notice when someone is hurting, missing, or in need. That's how we're to operate in God's family, as His children, as brothers and sisters.

We've been given a trust: each other. Our Father in heaven has asked us to watch out for each other, to love each other.

Look around. Is anyone missing?

"Where is your brother?"

A Moment of Introspection

- If you have kids, do they look out for each other? If so, how? If not, how would you like them to do so?
- Who are your brothers and sisters? What kinds of relationships do you have?
- Have any of your spiritual brothers or sisters "wandered off"? If so, how can you reach out to them?

13

"*Hold my hand.*"

"Hold my hand. We're in a parking lot."

"I don't want to!"

"I didn't ask if you wanted to. Hold my hand. This is dangerous."

"I'll be okay."

"This is no time for an argument. This is time for obedience. You don't know the dangers I know. Hold my hand."

For some kids this conversation is never necessary. For others, it's a regular discourse.

With some children, you hold out your hand and they take it—no questions asked. For others, every extension of your hand represents a challenge to their independence, their identity. If you're a parent, you know what I know: Holding hands can be a security issue.

What's the deal? I just wanted to hold his hand. When did that become such a big deal?

What, are you afraid to be seen with me? Afraid of what someone might think? Afraid of who might think it isn't cool? All I wanted to do was hold your hand. Who knew it was going to turn into a debate?

Parking lots make me very nervous. Besides the fact that so many use them as mini-racetracks, they're peppered with little kids who are at the mercy of drivers. You know the ones I'm talking about—the ones who refuse to hold hands with their parents. These kids are short, difficult to see, and perfectly unpredictable. They hop, skip, and dart. They practice walking backward or with their eyes shut, just for fun. They're completely oblivious to the surrounding dangers.

Their parents often walk way in front of them. The only thing I can figure is that Mom and Dad don't want to witness the inevitable. They've given up on holding their child's hand and guiding him or her. They've spoken their piece: "If you get hit by a car, don't come running to me!"

Jesus wants me to take His hand, His nail-scarred hand, and walk with Him through life. He wants me to take His hand because I love Him.

When I was little I loved going to church with my Nana Burt. I loved to hear her sing the old hymns. I loved the Juicy Fruit gum she always had for me during the sermon. And I loved holding her hand.

Often during the service I would rub lotion on her hands. Even now, Jergen's lotion brings back sweet memories. I loved to look at the veins and wrinkles in her hands; when I pinched one of her wrinkles it would stay like that for a while, which I thought was so cool.

Most of all I would imagine all the things her hands had

done. She was a gardener, a seamstress, a wife, a mother. Those hands had seen many a weed and bug. They'd been pricked with many pins and needles, burned on her hot stove. She'd caressed and bathed and spanked and patted and crocheted and folded with those hands. As a little girl she'd picked cotton, and those hands had bled. Her hands told the story of her life. I still love to sit and hold my Nana's hands, those hands that have loved me and others so well.

Jesus extends His hand for me to hold every day. And as He does, I remember His story. On that hand is the sweet smell of carpenter's oil. His hands are the ones that restored sight, lifted up the lame, and broke the bread. They cracked the whip in the Temple courts and reverently unrolled scrolls in the synagogue. They touched the untouchables, comforted the hopeless, washed the feet of His disciples, and stretched out on a cross as if to say, "I love you this much!"

His hands are not soft, but the rough hands of a wood-worker, calloused over time, beyond blistering. They are also scarred eternally as a reminder of the punishment that should have been mine. These are no ordinary hands.

Yet sometimes when He offers one for me to hold, I refuse. Instead of jumping at the chance to walk with my Savior, Master, and King, I glance around and wonder, *What would everyone else think? What if they saw me holding His hand? It might make me look like a wimp. What if they thought I really needed Him, that I couldn't handle it all on my own? And those scars—I don't want to see those. Why do I have to see where the nails were?*

"Come on, Rachael," He gently whispers. "Hold My hand.

I want you to know that you are never alone. I want to remind you that I am faithful and true. I want you to know My power, remember My sacrifice, and imitate My service. I do not want you to hold My hand because you have to, but because you want to. I will not make you. But I'm ready when you are. Hold My hand."

A Moment of Introspection

- When is it important for you to hold your child's hand? Why?
- When would you most like to hold God's hand? Are you usually willing to take it or are you resistant? Why?
- Do you ever substitute someone else's hand for the hand of God? If so, what would you like to do about that?

14

"Be careful."

R emember the old song from nursery class in church? "Be careful, little hands, what you do . . ."

I remember all the verses. It's a simple song that continues to minister to my heart and to the hearts of my children.

"Be careful" has to be on the top ten list of things I most often say:

"Be careful of the fire ant pile!"

"Be careful of the slippery ice!"

"Be careful of the edge of the cliff!"

"Be careful of the traffic!"

My kids usually go through life enjoying every step, oblivious to danger, just having fun. When I say, "Be careful!" they look at me as if to say, "Of what?"

Every parent who's ever watched her newly licensed driver take the keys for the first time and head out on his own knows what I'm talking about. "Be careful," we say.

"Yeah, yeah. See you later," the fledgling driver answers. Or a simple, "I will, Mom." It does little to calm our nerves.

Shortly after I got my license, my mother tried to explain all of her "Be carefuls." "It is not you that I am worried about," she would say. "It's all of those other loons out on the road!"

It made me feel better that she wasn't questioning me—though today she confesses it was really the other drivers *and* me that made her nervous.

We come to know dangers from experience. But how can we tell our kids without scaring them? Usually we try to summarize with a simple, "Be careful."

Molly hits her brother. "Be careful, little hands, what you do."

Anderson speaks an unkind word. "Be careful, little mouth, what you say."

Charles carelessly searches on the Internet. "Be careful, little eyes, what you see."

Savannah Anne goes somewhere without permission. "Be careful, little feet, where you go."

It's so easy to apply the song to someone else—but it's for me, too. The verse that most applies to me is, "Be careful, little mind, what you think." This is important because there is a battle for our minds. That is why we're commanded to "set your minds on things above" (Colossians 3:2).

I have to guard myself against wrong thinking, the lies of the surrounding culture, thoughts and questions like, "What about me? When can I do what I want to do? Who is looking out for me? I deserve this. I would be happier if . . ."

For this reason, I have to be careful how I spend my free time.

This may sound funny coming from a mother of seven. Most people probably think I don't even know what free time is. But I do, and value it. Unfortunately, I sometimes waste it with meaningless "stuff." Instead of using my time to meditate on His truth, I watch TV or slip into gossip with a friend. During those moments God whispers, "Be careful."

I need to be careful where I go, what I do, what I watch, what I read, who I talk to, and what I think—because those actions affect my relationship with God. He knows that so many things He wants me to be careful of can easily turn into sin. He knows they can and will lead to my destruction.

The words from that simple childhood song are so poignant still. I say an unkind word; I roll my eyes at a sister; I leaf through another catalog. God wants me to be careful because of the dangers I do not see.

Because He loves me, He says, "Be careful."

A Moment of Introspection

- If you have kids, what do you want them to be careful of? Why?
- What does it mean to be discerning? How are you learning discernment and teaching it to your children?
- Are there habits with which you've grown comfortable, but which might be dangerous? If so, what should you do?

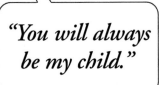

15

"You will always be my child."

A s I hold and rock little Benjamin, I stroke his precious cheeks. He's such a content baby. Yet already he's grown so much, no longer the little seven-pounder he was upon his arrival. He reminds me of how fast it all goes.

I look at Charles, my firstborn. At 14 he's about as tall as I am, which means taller is right around the corner. Anderson, who took his time learning to talk, now loves to discuss a variety of subjects.

Both boys still like to sit in my lap from time to time and just snuggle. I can't turn them down. I remember when they were much smaller and we would snuggle and wrestle on the floor and they would belly-laugh.

As I witness their transformation into young men, it's from an awesome perspective. They will always be my two little boys running and jumping in a pile of raked leaves. I will always remember them trying to catch a lizard on the front porch, and squirting each other with their water guns. I have memories of hornet stings, cuts with stitches, hurt feelings, laughter, and tears.

My two boys have big dreams—dreams that, when fulfilled,

will take them far from me. Dreams given to them by the Dream Giver. Dreams of being torchbearers for Him. But no matter how far they go, how tall they grow, or what they pursue, they will always be my boys.

When I was growing up, my mother gave me a unique perspective on newsmakers. When a "Most Wanted" picture flashed on the evening news, she would comment, "That is someone's little boy."

Somehow it made that man look different. He seemed less like a hardened criminal and more like a lost little boy. Somewhere there was a mother who would love to take him into her arms and tell him that she loved him. At least that was how it went in my daydream. He would always be her child.

Having accepted the gift of Christ's sacrifice as payment for my sin, I am God's child. I don't always act like a king's daughter. But He says, "You will always be my child—even though you may not choose to act like it today."

Did you catch that? He loves me no matter what. "Who shall separate us from the love of Christ? . . . For I am convinced that neither death nor life, neither angels nor demons, neither the present nor the future, nor any powers, neither height nor depth, nor anything else in all creation, will be able to separate us from the love of God that is in Jesus Christ our Lord" (Romans 8:35, 38-39).

Understanding this brings peace and security. Just as I cannot do anything to earn or deserve His love, grace, or forgiveness, I will always be His child. If we confess our sins, He is faithful and just to forgive us our sins (1 John 1:9). He removes our sins as far as the east is from the west (Psalm 103:12). His mercies are new every morning! (Lamentations 3:22-23)

Our sonship is not based on our perfection, but on His perfect sacrifice. It is not based on our own strength, but His resurrection power. It is not based on our deeds, but on His.

In short, our Father's grace, love, forgiveness, mercy, and power surpass any of our confessed sins. He is the great Redeemer, able to make good on our bad choices.

If you have received His Son as Savior, He is your Father. Wherever you are, whatever you've been up to, He wants you to know, "You will always be My child."

A Moment of Introspection

- If you're a parent, what do you remember about your children when they were babies? Toddlers? Preschool age? School-aged? Teenagers?
- How can you communicate to your kids the idea that they will always be your children?
- If you belong to Christ, do you remember when you first became God's child? What was it like? How do you feel about the idea of always being His child?

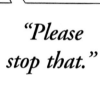

"*Please
stop that.*"

16

B anging out "Chopsticks" on the piano for the 43rd time.
"Please stop that."

"Can I have another cookie? Pleeeeaaaassssse?"

"Please stop that."

"Smack, munch, smack, munch . . ."

"Please stop that."

Wet towels on the bed—again.

"Please stop that."

Arguing with a sibling.

"Please stop that."

And on and on . . .

There are things my kids do that aren't wrong, but have the capacity to push me over the edge. When that happens, I plead, "Please stop that!"

It's important to deal with these irritants, as they can affect relationships—even if they're only of the "knuckle popping" variety. I mean habits like incessantly popping one's knuckles or drumming one's fingers on a table. These are of no eternal significance, but they sure are annoying.

Then there are behaviors that *do* have eternal significance. The need to stop them goes way beyond how much they bother me. They bother God because they're sins. Lying, stealing, cheating, rudeness, and hate have to be dealt with. They matter in the long run; they matter forever.

While correcting one of my children, I often find my heavenly Father softly whispering to me, "Please stop that. Please stop avoiding Me. Please stop gossiping about your sister. Please stop over-committing. Please stop spending all the money on yourself. Please stop complaining. Please stop wasting the time I have given you on the Internet. Please stop."

Sometimes we have to stop what we're doing in order to start being all that God has planned for us to be.

Recently Davis and I had a great day planned for the kids. Wanting to surprise them, we hadn't outlined it. But we had plans to bless them.

Unfortunately, their impatience got the best of them. They started bickering; they were lazy; they wasted time. Soon the plans we'd made to enjoy the day together turned into a course of training and discipline. We had to review lessons and behaviors that we'd gone over and over before. As parents we couldn't proceed with the blessing until the behavior was right. Our kids had to "please stop that" before the blessings could be bestowed.

God wants us to "please stop that" and start acting like His children. He wants us to start loving each other, extend grace to each other, and serve one another.

At least some of the things I want so desperately for my kids to stop are things that *I* haven't stopped, at least not completely. When I realize that my husband and I are the two most influential role models our children have, that's overwhelming. Maybe that's why God uses them to show me my sin.

It's easy to grow accustomed to the sins in my life. But when they show up in my children, they seem hideous; I seek immediately to "please stop" them. That's one way my heavenly Father gets my attention.

A Moment of Introspection

- If you have children, what do you find yourself asking them to stop? Why?
- Are you balancing "Stop that" with "Keep up the good work"? If not, how could you do that this week?
- What might God like you to stop doing in order to carry out His plans for you? What might He want you to *start* doing?

17

> "Follow the directions."

For most of my life I tried to avoid reading and following directions. I'm not sure why, except that I guess I thought I could figure it out on my own, thank you very much.

But I've come to appreciate directions and strive to follow them as much as possible. I think some of this comes with parenthood.

My son Charles loves to bake. One day he wanted to bake a pound cake. He'd made banana bread, rolls, cookies, and other kinds of cakes, but never a pound cake. He looked through all my cookbooks and found a recipe that sounded good.

"Can I make it?" he asked.

"Sure," I answered.

To know Charles is to know that he's passionate about all he does. He never attempts something halfway. I could hear the sounds of his work coming from the kitchen: the refrigerator door opening and closing, the cabinet doors slamming, the cracking of eggs, the mixer, the occasional "Oops!" and "Uh-oh." He even whistled as he worked.

Finally he greased the pans, poured in the batter, placed his masterpieces in the oven, and set the timer. All he had to do was wait an hour—and it would take at least that long to clean up the disaster area he'd created in the kitchen.

Lacking enthusiasm for the cleaning task, he concentrated on constantly checking his project. Finally the timer sounded, marking the end of "cooking time" and the beginning of "eating time," as he put it.

The cakes smelled awesome. Kids came from all over the house to investigate and request a piece, but the cakes had to cool. Eventually Charles got the first taste. But it wasn't good.

It seems that pound cake doesn't work if made with substitute ingredients. When the recipe calls for butter, it means butter—not margarine or butter-flavored Crisco.

Charles hadn't followed the directions. He'd made a substitution, skipping the recipe's advice to the contrary. And he was disappointed with the results.

He thought the substitutions would make the pound cake "good enough." But the person who wrote the recipe knew better than Charles did.

The person who wrote that recipe didn't set up the directions to frustrate Charles or anyone else. She just knew what would work and what wouldn't.

Likewise, God has set forth directions for living. He knows the ingredients necessary to live extraordinary lives full of meaning and excitement as we seek Him. But too often we think a few little substitutions here or there won't make any difference. And they won't—on the outside.

We may look the same to everyone else, but our hearts won't

be as He wants them to be. If we neglect His directions, we'll be disappointed with the results. Worse, we may blame Him for our frustration.

Take parenting, for instance. The Bible includes many directives on this subject. One of the most specific is in Ephesians 6:4: "Do not exasperate your children." This is directed to fathers, but is important for mothers, too. It's also one I really struggle with.

When my kids do something wrong, I want to launch into a sermonette. I want to give them a passionate speech, to be witty, clever, and pointed. Sometimes I even slip into sarcasm and am harsh and hurtful.

How shocking can it be when they respond to me or a sibling in the same way? I've trained them well, having been a strong example of exasperation. The figurative "pound cake" of our family may look good, but it tastes awful.

I have only myself to blame, as I made a substitution on His recipe. I didn't follow His directions.

Too often I'm like Charles. Enthusiastic about following Christ, I get into doing a bunch of stuff for Him. The flour is flying in the kitchen; I make noise as I take shortcuts around His directions and forge ahead in my own strength.

But God's ultimate goal is not any project or ministry. It's my relationship with Him.

Do I trust Him enough to follow His directions, even if they don't seem to make sense? Do I obey when He says, "No substitutions"?

Am I willing to follow His directions?

A Moment of Introspection

- If you're a parent, do your kids like to follow directions? What are some directions you'd like them to follow more closely?
- How do you model following directions?
- What biblical directions could you share with your children today?

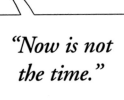

*"Now is not
the time."*

18

B efore breakfast: "Can I have some of my Valentine's candy?" The afternoon before the evening wedding: "Can we play in the sandbox?"

At the dinner table with neighbors: "Last week we all had the stomach flu. We . . ."

When I've just sat down to nurse the baby: "Can you show me how to do this cross-stitch?"

Sometimes I want to respond by saying, "Are you kidding? Are you aware of the time? Do you remember what we're trying to accomplish here?"

But my kids don't. They haven't even noticed the dots on the page, much less connected them.

I believe my children genuinely don't see the problem with these requests. They must be taught to think of their requests in the context of the whole picture. Even then they won't always understand why "Now is not the time." But they'll have to accept the answer.

It's not that I'll never allow them to have their Valentine's Day candy, or play in the sandbox, or tell stories about all of us throwing up, or teach them to cross-stitch. Now is just not the time for it.

The reasons can vary widely. It may simply not be in a child's best interest to do that activity now. Or the activity may demand more time, skill, or supplies than I currently have. Or I might have that activity planned for another time.

"Not now" isn't "No." It's more like "Later." Of course, that may not satisfy a child. It doesn't help that we live in such an instant society—instant Internet access, instant oatmeal, instant coffee, instant potatoes.

"What do you mean, 'Now is not the time'?" In our culture it seems that now is the time for whatever you want it to be the time for.

In the Bible there are many occasions on which God answered, in effect, "Now is not the time." Sometimes He said this so that there could be no mistaking who was at work. Often His divine delays made it clear that He is the only One who deserves the glory. Sometimes the purpose was to show up the enemy as much as it was to remind God's people of His power and might.

Does this mean that when we call out to Him, He doesn't listen? That it doesn't matter? Of course not. While we're waiting, He is working on us—to perfect us into His Son's likeness. He has to work in us to rid us of ourselves.

He is the Master of timing, wanting it to be perfect. It probably won't seem perfect to us. But there is my timing, and all the other options I can think of, even the ones I don't like—and then there is His timing.

I think that sometimes God hears my inappropriate request and wants to say to me, "Rachael, what are you thinking? Honey, now is just not the time for that. I know you want it bad and I know you want it now and I know you think you have it all figured out. But hang tough; we've got some work to do. If you'll just trust Me on the timing, you'll see that Mine was better."

I usually have it all planned—how I want a situation to go. Often I assume it will go that way. After all, I thought it all through, made my charts and graphs, weighed pros and cons, made decisions. The time has come to go forward. But in all my planning, charting, and stressing, I leave something—or rather Someone—out.

When God answers me with "Now is not the time," it's pretty upsetting. I start in with a good "Why?" and "Come on, now!"

He must be amused when I try to talk Him into my plan. I want to move, sell a house, change churches, end a friendship, take a vacation, have a child, or write a book.

"Now is not the time," comes His reply.

A Moment of Introspection

- If you're a parent, what's your most embarrassing "bad timing" story involving your kids?
- When has your timing been wrong while His was right?
- How can you best spend your time waiting for the right time?

"*Share!*"

19

S̲ avannah Anne had it first; it was hers. But Elizabeth took it without asking when Savannah Anne set it down for a moment.

This time it was a doll, but it could have been anything. The important thing was "who had it."

All morning Savannah Anne had been dressing her doll up in new outfits she'd gotten for her birthday. All morning Elizabeth had watched and waited and asked to try some of the clothes on her own doll. Elizabeth had been turned down— kindly, but repeatedly.

Impatient, Elizabeth had gone for the whole enchilada; she'd taken the doll. Now she had sister's attention.

Once she had the doll, Elizabeth no longer was interested in the outfits. Guess where she went next, with big sister following closely at her heels?

Both girls sat down close to where I was working. Savannah Anne started the conversation. "Mom, Elizabeth took my doll," she said.

There was no response from Elizabeth. She just sat there

with the doll, apparently thinking she knew what was coming next.

"Savannah Anne, why do you think she took the doll?" I asked.

They seemed surprised at my question. I could almost hear Savannah Anne thinking, *Who cares why? Aren't you supposed to tell her not to take without asking? It's my doll! I had it! I only put it down for a second. She has her own doll!*

Finally she answered, "I don't know."

"I think you do know," I said. "Think about it. What have you been doing all morning? What are you usually doing this time every day?"

"I am usually playing with my sisters. And I am."

"Are you?" I asked. "I think you are playing with your doll, and your sister is feeling left out."

"Oh," she replied.

"See, this time her grabbing is related to your not sharing. It is not always like this, but this time it is. You could have prevented this by sharing. She had asked and you did not respond. She thought that you were not listening, so she did something to get you to take her seriously. I think her plan worked."

Elizabeth was trying to hide her smile, looking glad that someone had explained the situation.

"Now . . . is grabbing the right way to get what you want?" I asked Elizabeth.

"No, Ma'am," she said.

"Girls, do you think that you could go and work this out together? Do you think that you could consider the other person as you work this out? If you need me, I am right here. I would be happy to help you."

They were off to their room, where giggles echoed.

God has made me a steward of everything I have. He's given it to me for sharing. Not to let it collect dust, not to horde, not to waste, not to flaunt—but to share.

That's the joy of it all, sharing. Alas, some things are easier to share than others. Some things are more dear or fragile or important.

Not always, but often, sharing and grabbing are related. If I don't share, someone grabs. Or if someone else doesn't share, I grab.

When my kids act out such impatience and selfishness on life's stage, I say, "Share!"

When I'm the actor, God gives me similar direction.

A Moment of Introspection

- If you're a parent, how do you handle it when your kids aren't interested in sharing?
- How long is the list of things you're unwilling to share? Would it depend on who was asking? Why?
- How is hospitality a form of sharing? What's hardest about it for you?

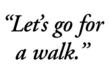

> ## "Let's go for a walk."

G oing for a walk is one of my favorite things to do with my children.

It's a great way to start off our day together or wrap it up before bed. It's a great way to take a break from a rough or tiring day, and it can energize a disappointing one.

We've learned not to leave on our walks without a "critter keeper." After all, you never know what you might find. Over the years we've caught some pretty amazing things—lizards, turtles, and snakes (the small, nonvenomous kind). Anderson maintains an amazing bug chart full of insects, many of which were found on our strolls. And that's without mentioning the beautiful or unusual leaves, rocks, twigs, and bark we've collected.

It's also become our habit on these walks to point out God to each other.

"Oh, children, look what God has done," I say as I notice a perfectly spun spider's web.

"Look at the colors God used to paint the sky tonight!" one of the children might say, looking at the sunset.

As we walk, we discuss current events. And we discuss God in the context of His creation.

"How did He do that?" Molly might ask, referring to a beautiful rock she found.

Or Elizabeth, when asked, "Who did that?" will exclaim, "Jesus!"

Through our walks, the Creator becomes tangible as they see the work of His hands. We leave all the "stuff" at home and relax with Him; He wows us with His creation. Somehow the squabbling and discontentment melt away as we walk with the Master. It's a reminder of what's really important and *who's* in control.

At the end of a bad day—when I'm beyond my patience, when nothing has seemed to go right, and frustration has been the order of the day—God whispers, "Let's go for a walk."

"I can't," I reply, annoyed.

I think He must not know what I'm going through. He should know not to ask me to go for a walk.

But He does know, and that's why He asks.

He wants to get me outside, away from it all. He wants to remind me who He is. He wants me to "be still and know."

All I want to do on days like this is crawl under the covers or turn on the TV. But He wants more for me. The bed and sleep wouldn't bring the comfort He can, and the television would only put off resolving issues by numbing and distracting me.

God wants to help and heal me. He wants to hear my heart as we walk together. He's big enough to hear me ramble on about what I'm feeling.

When he says, "Let's go for a walk," taking Him up on His offer is an act of trust on my part. It's saying "yes" to Him and His wisdom. It's choosing His perfect peace in the middle of the storm. It's putting my relationship with Him first and not substituting a cheap imitation.

All along the way it's as though He whispers, "So, tell Me all about it. Hey, did you see that flower? I know that you love flowers. I made this one with you in mind. Do you see the details in the petals? And isn't that your favorite color? Oh, Rachael, I love you so much. I know about all you are going through. Just like that flower, I know and I have a plan. Take a deep breath and trust Me."

Have you had a bad day? Need a break? Wish Calgon could take you away? How about a walk? Why not stroll outside and take in a fresh view of who He is and what He's made?

Notice how orderly His creation is. When things are confused and chaotic at our house, He draws me outside. In His creation is harmony. There are no birds crashing into the ground; they are not singing off-key; they are not attacking me. No, the birds in my neighborhood are flying to and fro, gathering food or fodder for their nests, singing as they work. Oh, the peace.

Some days my walk doesn't take me very far. I may have the energy to walk a couple of miles, but only enough time to go as far as the mailbox. On some days I don't even make it off the front porch.

But those moments in His creation refocus, reenergize, and rejuvenate me. When I return and close the door behind me, my perspective has changed—as His peace has descended.

A Moment of Introspection

- Do you like going for walks? Why or why not?
- If you have kids, when was the last time you went for a walk with them? Did you have opportunities to point your kids to the Creator?
- When have you gone on a walk alone with Him? When can you schedule your next one?

21

"Turn down the music!"

I used to love loud music in my car. I mean really loud—shake-the-car loud, drown-out-a-siren loud, can't-hear-a-horn-honking loud.

When I was young, I turned my radio up because it was cool to know the words to the songs and have them blaring at the intersection. I probably also did it as an escape from the responsibilities that nagged me—and as a kind of rebellion. My parents didn't care for the music, which was not God-honoring. They gave me speeches about hearing loss and emergency situations, the whole bit. Still I turned it up as loud as it would go.

My husband Davis tells how, when we were first married, he had to get into the habit of turning the radio volume knob down before turning the car on—so as not to blast his ears out.

Charles is definitely my son. He loves his contemporary Christian music and he loves it loud. Sometimes I think he wants the music on loud or not at all.

He has not learned to listen to his loud music while doing anything else. If the music is on, he—at least at some level—is off.

"Hello, Charles!" I have said at loud volume. "Hello!" He

sings with all his heart, totally into the song, oblivious to little Joseph tugging at his pant leg. "Charles, turn down the music!" I finally say.

"Mom, I like it loud," he replies.

"I need your attention. I do not want to compete with the radio."

Maybe for you the distraction isn't loud music; maybe it's television. I've struggled with that, too. Davis used to try talking to me when I was watching a show, but couldn't get a response. He'd make a game out of trying to get my attention by saying certain words or phrases like "tornado" or "throw up" or "emergency." Nothing worked. I would think, *I'm into my show. Why is he trying to distract me, anyway? Can't it just wait? The show doesn't have much longer.*

These days, things have changed. Davis doesn't have to prepare his ears for a loud car radio anymore. With seven kids, I love the idea of silence. There are days and even weeks when the television isn't on at our house.

Still, I sometimes can hear God whisper, "Rachael, turn down the music." The music can be anything that distracts me from His voice—radio, television, movies, books, e-mail, catalogs, magazines. It can even be "Christian."

God doesn't want me distracted. He doesn't want to compete with my shows. He wants all my attention, not part of it.

The more stuff we turn down, or off, the more clearly we'll be able to hear Him. He wants us to turn it down and tune into Him. He's not silent as so many suppose. He's just getting drowned out.

When we open the ears of our hearts and listen, He speaks in a gentle whisper. He is best heard when the music is turned down.

Silence gives us opportunities to meditate on Scripture and linger in prayer. We can "be still and know" that He is God. We can reflect on His faithfulness or count our blessings. We can hear others, pray for those we love, think of ways to serve them.

Many want to hear from God, but expect Him to turn down the volume on the distractions around them. He doesn't work that way. It's your knob.

Want to hear from Him? Turn down the music.

A Moment of Introspection

- If you're a parent, do your children like to play their music loudly? What's their response if you ask them to turn it down?
- What are your top three distractions? Do you use them to drown anything out? If so, what?
- Where and when are you most likely to get some "peace and quiet"? How soon can you do that?

"Life isn't fair."

22

The pieces of cake aren't exactly the same size.

One brother is invited to a party; the other isn't.

The referee makes a bad call in the game.

"I know, life's not fair!"

And you know what? It's not. The great American myth is that life should be fair, even, equal, identical, the same for everyone.

What's your first reaction when your kids whine, "It's not fair!"? Mine, too. I want to say something like, "You're right! You've caught on! Welcome to the real world!"

But that's when something horrible happens. I start thinking about all the unfair things in *my* world. *It's not fair that they get to go on a cruise. It's not fair that they got a new car. It's not fair that she can eat all that chocolate without consequences.* I list all the reasons why I should have whatever it is I want. It's really petty, and ugly.

It's especially so when compared with that other list of "not fairs": *It's not fair that their daughter was diagnosed with leukemia. It's not fair that she had to die and leave her two children and hus-*

*band at such young ages. It's not fair that he decided he didn't want
to be married anymore and walked out on his family.*

No, it's not fair. In fact, it stinks.

When sin entered the world, so did unfairness. Sin affects
not only the sinner, but also the innocent. A drunk driver walks
away from an accident without a bruise, while the ambulance
delivers his victims to the morgue. A mother who longs to hold
her baby suffers another miscarriage, while an abusive mother
starves her child until he dies. A man who's worked hard all his
life loses his job—and health insurance and pension—when his
company files for bankruptcy.

It's not an illusion; it's not fair.

But this inequity doesn't mean God is not just. It means the
timing of His justice isn't ours. Ultimately, He will have justice
on behalf of His beloved bride. For now, in the midst of unfairness, we're to wait on Him and trust Him.

Our circumstances may appear uneven, but God loves each
of us equally. Love is the answer when life is not fair.

When my kids start in on "It's not fair," they're overlooking
everything else I've done for them, everything else I've given
them, all my love for them. When they whine about unfairness,
it reminds me that I do the same thing to my heavenly Father. It
happens when I lose my focus and ignore His blessings.

The character of Job in the Bible is one of the strongest
examples of how to handle life's unfairness. When everything
had been taken away from him without explanation, he fell on
his face and cried out, "The LORD gave and the LORD has taken
away; may the name of the LORD be praised" (Job 1:21).

Life isn't fair. But God is good and faithful all the time. We can choose which of these truths will trump the other.

Are we going to focus on the unfairness of it all, or on the goodness of God?

Are we going to blame Him, or bless His holy name?

A Moment of Introspection

- If you're a parent, how often do you or your children say, "That's not fair!"? What do your kids want you to do when they say it?
- In what area of your life do you feel things are most unfair? Who do you talk to about it? Who are you blaming?
- How might it help you to focus on God's blessings and His love for you this week?

23

"I know how you feel."

L ast winter on a chilly morning, I was sitting in a rocking chair near our glowing gas logs, nursing little Benjamin. This was not the first time we'd been together in the last few hours; smiles and yawns took turns on my face while Ben nursed and dozed. The rest of the family was asleep—or so I thought.

Suddenly two-year-old Joseph came in, all grins, hopping and skipping enthusiastically. "Hi, Ben!" he said.

Ben and I were both startled. I tried to hush Joseph, wondering why he wasn't sleeping—and where I could pick up some of his energy.

I told him not to go behind the rocker, but he darted there anyway. I wasn't in a position to grab him, and it was too late. In a flash he'd rubbed his arm against the frame of the fireplace insert and burned himself.

Now we were all up.

Joseph was really hurting. The burn was pretty big, extending from just above his elbow to halfway to his shoulder. His tears were big and his eyes grew red.

I felt so bad. There was little I could do for the pain, other than holding him and singing to him. Soon I was teary, too; we all were. I just wanted to say, "I know how you feel."

In this situation, I knew the danger—the physical threat of Joseph's skin coming in contact with the hot fireplace. He didn't. He was depending on me to protect him.

I, in turn, was counting on him to obey me—even if he didn't understand why. In the end, his mischievousness cost him.

Several months later, Joseph hasn't forgotten. When he walks by the fireplace—at a great distance—he usually says to no one in particular, "Hot!"

Sometimes my children get hurt because they're just playing around. They're ignorant of the risks, not realizing the problems with playing in the road, or in an old refrigerator, or around an abandoned well. I have to teach—and re-teach—them about danger and its consequences.

Even then they'll sometimes choose to take a risk. When that happens, it's not enough to deliver an "I told you so" or a mini-sermon on paying attention. Tears, hugs, and many an "I love you" are the order of the day.

Hurts can be emotional, too. One summer evening, at a party with friends, I watched as my kids had a great time. But then Savannah Anne showed up, her eyes red.

"What is it?" I asked.

Finally the tears came. "She called me stupid," she replied, referring to another girl.

"Oh, honey," I said, sitting down and bringing her into my lap. "I am so sorry. I have had people call me names, too. It really hurts. I know how you feel."

The only thing worse than my own pain is seeing my kids in pain. My instinct is to lash out in their defense, but that's not what they need at that moment. First I need to hug them and reassure them of my love.

I've experienced many kinds of pain in my life. There was physical pain when a friend thought it would be funny to move a mini-trampoline out from under me while I was jumping; landing on my tailbone put me in a lot of pain for several days. There was the emotional pain in junior high of being taller than all the boys and having huge feet.

Mom and I cried together through those years. She shared my pain; she hurt with me. Now, as a mom, I know some of what she felt watching me endure my trials.

There was a time when I thought God was indifferent to my pain. I thought He didn't care about the hurt as much as He did about my learning lessons and not repeating mistakes.

But He does! He longs to hold us and rock us as tears run down our cheeks. He knows how we feel.

Whenever I doubt it, I can remember that morning by the fireplace.

A Moment of Introspection

- If you're a parent, when was the last time you hurt for your child? How did you show your compassion?
- What is the biggest hurt in your life right now?
- Have you allowed God's love and compassion to wash over you? Why or why not?

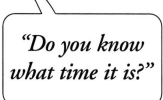

"*Do you know
what time it is?*"

24

I say this to my kids a lot—when they lose track of time and risk missing something important.

It's only funny when it happens to them, though. When it happens to me, it's embarrassing.

There are two times in my life when I can remember forgetting an appointment.

One was a couple of years ago when I'd volunteered to take dinner to a new mom. A dear friend gently reminded me by calling and asking, "Do you know what time it is?"

"Yes . . ." I responded slowly, not catching her clue. "It's dinner time."

"What are you having?" she asked, trying to let me figure it out.

"We are having . . ." Finally it hit me. "Oh, no! I was supposed to take dinner to Tina. I'll have to call and apologize or order pizza or something."

Tina was merciful; I was mortified.

The other time was much more recently. I was to be interviewed on the local Christian radio station to promote an upcoming retreat. The show's host, Gary, called; I was scheduled to come in the next Tuesday morning.

I told Davis, marked it on my calendar, and asked the retreat team to be praying.

When Tuesday morning came, Davis and I got up early as usual to spend time together reading the Bible and praying, then taking a brisk walk. Then, as Davis showered, I checked our voice messages.

Sure enough, there was one. It had been left at 7:16 A.M.

"Rachael, it's Gary . . ."

Gary? Oh, man, what time is it?

It was 7:46. A glance at the wall calendar reminded me: "WRCM interview 7 A.M."

Oh, man, what do I do?

There I was in all my stinky, sweaty, power-walked glory. Needless to say, I had to reschedule.

Gary was very understanding; I was chagrined.

"Do you know what time it is?" God asks me on occasion.

"It's time . . ." He continues, but I know where He's going.

It's time for me to tell that friend or co-worker about Jesus.

It's time for me to extend grace.

It's time for me to say, "I love you."

It's time for me to forgive.

It's time for me to get on with His business and stop allowing my unfinished business to steal my time and focus.

I have a very important appointment coming up. No one can determine the day or hour of Christ's return, but each moment brings me closer to that glorious event. It's time for me to stop putting things off, stalling, hoping problems will go away or solve themselves. It's time for me to be proactive, to "get my house in order" and prepare hearts for His kingdom.

Do you know what time it is?

When I forget, the Lord seems to tell me, "Oh, My child, you've gotten distracted and off course, and forgotten what time it is and what I have planned for you. Rachael, do you know what time it is? Please don't waste any more of it. I cannot tell you when yours will run out. I cannot tell you when I will return. The time has come for you to get on with all I have planned for you.

"It is time for you to realize that the time I have given you here matters in the end . . . and there is an end."

A Moment of Introspection

- If you're a parent, is there an activity in which your children lose all track of time? How could you help them with this?
- What time is it in your own life? What have you put off dealing with that needs to be done?
- How could praying and setting goals help you deal with the important things while there's still time?

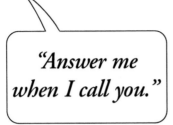

25

"*Answer me when I call you.*"

"Charles! Anderson! Savannah Anne! Molly! Elizabeth! Joseph!" I called. "Dinner!"

Time passed. I repeated the call. More time passed. I became concerned.

They were supposed to be at the pond. They had the walkie-talkie; why weren't they answering? Again I shouted. Again I tried the walkie-talkie.

Still more time passed. Davis arrived home. "Where are the kids?" he asked.

"They were supposed to be at the pond, fishing," I said. "I have tried them on the walkie-talkie and I have just tried calling them. They are not answering."

Davis tried both. No answer.

Just as Davis was preparing to walk to the pond himself, the kids walked in. They were all talking at once about their adventures.

But I wasn't interested in anything except why they were not listening to my voice when I called. What had distracted them?

Did they not hear me? Were they unaware of how it concerns me when they don't answer?

The kids explained that they'd heard my voice. They'd heard Dad's voice, too. But they were busy.

Besides, hadn't I told them they could be at the pond until 5:30? According to their watches, they still had 20 minutes when my first call came. They figured I was just calling to check in, nothing important. Since everything was okay, they just came at 5:30.

"But no matter what the original plan was, when we call, you must answer," Davis explained. "What if it had been an emergency and we had needed you home? What if something had happened to you and we were just calling to check in, but you were in danger? Answer your mother and me when we call you."

"Yes, sir."

Oh, I want to hear from God. I want to hear Him speak my name, to call on me. But too often I wander off to the pond. I get sidetracked with skipping stones and ignore His call.

I bait my line and start to fish; He calls again. But I think He doesn't really need me yet and I keep on fishing. I'll catch up with Him later, at my next quiet time or Bible study or Sunday morning worship.

But what if He needs me now?

Well, now is not convenient for me. I have other things to do—fish and turtles to catch, stones to skip and geese to watch. And I haven't been to the playground lately.

Sometimes when I hear from God, I don't answer. Why? Because I'm afraid.

I'm afraid He wants me to do something I don't want to do, like minister to a friend. I'm afraid He's found me out on some issue, like last week when I lied to make myself look better.

If I knew what He was going to say, I would consider answering. I want Him to say what I want to hear, not what He needs to say. I want Him to say that I've been doing really great lately, that my pride is justified, that my selfish actions are acceptable in light of the situation.

Basically, if there is something in it for me, I'll answer. Just like my kids.

God wants me, and you, to answer when He calls us—the first time. He wants us to be listening for His voice, ready to respond.

"Answer Me when I call you." We should answer for the simple reason that He is God—the one and only.

A Moment of Introspection

- If you're a parent, how do your kids respond when you call them? How would you like them to respond?
- Would you say you're listening for God's call? If so, what would you like to hear Him say? How does that compare with what you think He really wants to say?
- How can you listen more intently for His voice?

26

> ## "It doesn't matter what everyone else is doing."

"But Mom, everybody is wearing these!"
"Mom, everyone will be there."
"No one else has to do that."
"Everyone has seen it and said it was great!"
"How could so many other people be wrong?"

The answer to that last question is, "Very easily!"

When confronted with the outlandish things our children throw into this category, it's often easy for us to say, "No." Most of us have heard the classic response: "So if Johnny jumped off a cliff, would you do that, too?"

As protectors of our children, we can help them avoid getting caught up in the crowd and wasting their time, money, focus, and talents. We also can set standards for raising them that are based on God's plan for their lives.

The world has a standard, too, but its bar is much lower. The world says to do whatever makes you feel good, whatever makes you happy, or whatever everyone else is doing. These criteria assume your needs and wants are all-important.

In this day of "tolerance," we followers of Christ often

become wishy-washy in the name of being sensitive. We grow insensitive to the things that are important to Him—things like honesty and purity and boldness. But sometimes following Him means sticking out. Being different—the very thing that makes us so uncomfortable—can draw others to Him.

For example, the world says siblings aren't supposed to get along. They're supposed to taunt each other, aggravate each other, and generally get on each other's nerves. It says parents are supposed to dread the teenage years and look forward to the empty nest when they can get their lives back. But we're to be different. Both siblings and parents are called to love, selflessness, honesty, humility, and service. It doesn't matter what everyone else is doing!

As the song says, "They will know we are Christians by our love." Living out 1 Corinthians 13 will make us different enough that others will want to know why. When they ask, we're to have an answer prepared "for the hope that [we] have" (1 Peter 3:15).

Our challenge is simple, but difficult: We must quit caring what everyone else is doing and focus on what God has prepared for us to do. We must spend less time worrying about sticking out and more time seeking Him.

God cares what everyone else is doing. He cares so much that He sent His only Son to die on a cross for our sins while we were still sinning! Living out what we believe gives us an opportunity to lead more people to Him.

Either Christ has made a difference in our lives, or He hasn't. People should be able to tell the difference—and it should make them want to be different, too.

A Moment of Introspection

- If you have kids, you probably don't want them to do something just because someone else is doing it. On what *do* you want them to base their actions and beliefs?
- On what are *your* actions based? What are you doing because "everyone else is"?
- What are you neglecting to do because of what "everyone else" might think?

27

> **"You make
> me smile."**

T he kids were learning the fine art of joke telling. Four-year-old Elizabeth, wanting to get into the conversation, took a stab at telling one, too.

"I am going to tickle you!" she declared.

She knew it had something to do with getting people to laugh.

Her siblings looked at me for my reaction, and I burst out with a great big smile. Wondering whether they'd missed the punch line, some started laughing—which made us all grin. Elizabeth, meanwhile, grew a couple of inches.

My kids make me smile—especially when I see them loving and serving each other. I'm still in the process of teaching them to do that, and anticipate being so for the duration. But when I notice them being kind or living the Golden Rule, I can't help grinning.

One morning I took an important phone call. After becoming engrossed in the conversation, I realized there was silence in our house. When I stepped into the family room, there were no children to be seen.

Usually things get really loud when I'm on the phone, even though the kids "know better." *Hmmm,* I thought. *Should I investigate? This could be serious.*

I hung up the phone and followed my ears to the girls' room. There sat Anderson on the bed, surrounded by all his sisters, reading books to them! That made me smile—and cry. He was getting it!

Smiles can happen any time, whether or not I'm looking for them. Like during nap time. Or when Molly notices the laundry on the sofa and decides to fold it. Or when I catch Charles patiently playing LEGOs with Joseph. Or when Savannah Anne writes notes to people she loves. Or when little Benjamin squeals. Then there are smiles all around!

I want my kids to know that I enjoy them, everything about them. I like just being with them, listening to them talk, hearing them laugh, watching them play—especially together. I want them to remember me laughing and smiling, not scolding and glaring.

For them to have these memories, I have to make them daily realities. I need to smile at my kids and even throw in a wink, or a thumbs-up, or an "I love you" in sign language. They need the security that my smile brings. There'll be time enough for tears and stares, weariness and frustration. I must take every opportunity to smile at them and with them.

My smile should come easily. They shouldn't have to work for it or perform for it. It should be the rule, not the exception. It should represent how I feel about them as my children and as children of the King.

I grew up facing crowds, literally and figuratively. At those times I knew that if I could just catch a glimpse of my parents smiling at me, I'd be able to do whatever I was attempting—a basketball free throw, a speech tournament, a drama production, waiting on tables, raising a two-year-old, or facing personal challenges. Their smile meant they believed in me, were behind me, supported me, loved me.

God wants me to know that I make Him smile. He's there to support me no matter what I'm facing. He loves me. When I lean on Him, seek Him, honor Him, obey Him, or praise Him, I make Him smile.

Sometimes He may smile through heavenly tears as He witnesses my struggle to trust Him amid the storms of life. He knows I don't understand, but that I'm determined by His strength to do what He's said.

He is not a stern cosmic giant who stares down from on high, shooting angry looks at our every misstep or mistake. No, as He watches me grow into the person He created me to be, I can almost hear Him smile!

A Moment of Introspection

- If you're a parent, what does your child do that makes you smile?
- How many times a day do you suppose you smile at your children? How might they answer this question?
- What do you do that might make your heavenly Father smile?

28

"*No.*"

I once heard a mother say she didn't want to correct her son because she didn't want to be the bad guy.

She thought saying "No" would damage her relationship with the boy. Whenever possible, she explained, she put that responsibility on someone else. She wanted her son to remember her saying "Yes."

I was blessed with a mother who felt differently. She had a standard list of no's that were not up for discussion—things like motorcycles, tattoos, and bikinis. I not only inherited that list and passed it on to my own kids, but have added a few new ones.

The most important one I've added is "No reptiles in the house." I try to be a good sport about all the little critters my kids catch. In fact, I have caught my share of tree frogs, spiders, and caterpillars. I even like to hold an occasional snake, but I don't want them in the house.

Some of us think "No" hurts too much to say. I'd suggest that if we don't say it, we don't love enough.

Country singer Garth Brooks once recorded a song entitled, "Sometimes I Thank God for Unanswered Prayer." The implication is that some prayers are ignored, but that's not true. God answers all our prayers. It's just that when He says "No," we choose to hear nothing. We prefer to think He didn't answer, not that He answered in a way we didn't like.

For two years we tried earnestly to sell our house. The first year it was on the market, we didn't have one showing. That may seem like a crystal-clear answer to our prayers, but it wasn't the answer we wanted. So we put the house back on the market; after 6 months, 20 showings, and no offers, it became clear that God was answering—just not in the way we'd hoped.

We wanted to sell our house and build another for reasons that seemed good and right and selfless—like enabling our grandmothers to come for extended visits. But the answer was still "No."

What about you? What have you asked God for, only to get a "No"? A job promotion? A friend or relative to be healed? A relationship to be mended?

I believe most of our struggles come from failing to understand the "No."

"Why not?" we respond.

Isn't that just like our kids? They often don't understand our no's either. Even when we try to explain, the "Why?" question lingers.

It frustrates me that my kids won't just trust me and not question. I wish they'd review how faithful and dependable I've been to provide for all their needs. Maybe God feels that way about us.

The Ten Commandments are filled with the words "no" and

"not." Many people resent the list of "don'ts." Yet the Commandments were written by a sovereign, loving, gracious Father who wants to protect His children from unnecessary hurt.

God said "No" to His only begotten Son. In the Garden of Gethsemane Jesus begged His Father for another way to save mankind. But ultimately Jesus surrendered to His Father's will.

Sometimes we linger on our knees, pleading, long after an answer has come—because we don't like the answer. Like our children, we try to get God to rethink His "No." But when we get an answer, the next step we take should be toward obedience, not debate.

Remember the mother who wanted her son to recall her saying "Yes" and never "No"? She may achieve her goal. But I don't believe her son will respect or trust her as he would if she'd had the strength to say "No."

Sometimes our heavenly Father tells us "No," and sometimes there is no explanation. At those times we must reflect on His past faithfulness and love for us, and rest in the assurance of it.

In other words, we need to respond to His "No" the way we wish our kids would—in complete trust, and even gratitude.

A Moment of Introspection

- If you're a parent, when do you find yourself saying "No" to your kids?
- What are some requests you've made of your heavenly Father to which He has answered "No"?
- How could you praise Him in spite of His "No"?

29

> *"This is going to hurt me more than it's going to hurt you."*

We had it all planned. Davis was going to take the boys out for pizza, followed by a professional soccer game—a real "boys' night out." The girls and I were going to watch something really girly like *Beauty and the Beast*. We might even have a tea party.

But then it happened.

One of the boys lied about cleaning his room. He actually stuffed his clothes like sardines under the bed.

What had to happen next was obvious: It was going to be a boys' night out minus one. Neither Davis nor I wanted to enforce this one, but we had to.

Davis and one son still went out for pizza and the game; the girls and I watched Belle sing and dance while we ate popcorn. But there was a profound emptiness to the evening.

We'd wanted to see our son enjoy all we'd planned. It hurt us more than it hurt him, but I'm sure you couldn't have convinced him of that!

As a child, I never believed my parents were in pain when they lovingly served up discipline. I was convinced that at some level they enjoyed it. But then I saw them cry; I realized my disobedience had hurt them, and that they'd wanted me to enjoy the rewards of obedience. My foolish choices hurt us both.

When I punish my kids, it hurts me because I know the big picture. I know about the rewards they could experience. When they blow it, we both lose. Amazingly, I lose more—because I know what could have been.

So it is with our heavenly Father. He wants to bless us by doing immeasurably more than anything we can ask or imagine (Ephesians 3:20). When we blow it, we get the opposite of what He'd planned for us.

There's an old preacher's story, one my dad told, of a saint arriving in heaven. He was welcomed by Peter and encouraged to explore the vast library. Curious, the man went to see if his life's story was included with the rest. Sure enough, he found it—or thought he had. It looked right at first—right birthday and place, right name—but there were discrepancies in what had happened.

Peter happened by and asked, "Well, what did you find?"

"I thought I found my life's story," the man said. "It starts out right, but then there are a bunch of things I never did."

"Oh," said Peter. "I must have forgotten to mention that these are the books that contain the life stories of what *could* have been, what the Master had planned. If you want to read about what actually happened, follow that hallway to where we keep the log of events."

Ephesians 2:10 says that we are God's workmanship, created to do good works which He prepared in advance. He knows the big picture. He anticipates our joy in fulfilling all He has planned, because it's what we were created to do.

Our sin hurts Him because there's no excuse for it. He's given us everything we need to succeed, and we choose failure.

Fortunately, He disciplines the sheep He loves. It's not always pleasant—for either of us. But those He trains will reap a harvest of peace and righteousness (Hebrews 12:11).

A Moment of Introspection

- If you're a parent, when have you had to discipline your kids by taking away something you were looking forward to? How did you feel?
- Was it harder for you or for them?
- Do you agree that disciplining you might be painful for God? Why or why not?

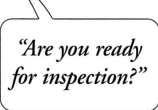

*"Are you ready
for inspection?"*

30

The kids and I have drastically different definitions of words like "clean" and "organized." I try to help them with both by providing things like hampers, notebooks, plastic bins, baskets, and file folders. Yet they still struggle.

On Saturdays we do a variety of tasks for the week ahead. The boys are supposed to clean out the car, organize their dresser drawers, and put away the week's last load of clean laundry. Then there's the playroom—the place where LEGOs multiply as does creativity. The kids don't have to destroy these creations, but I do ask them to clear a path on which to walk.

Before moving from one task to the next, they're supposed to ask for an inspection. But often they skip this important step, leaving Davis or me to ask the question: "Are you ready for inspection?"

"Inspection? Yes," they reply.

"Did you remember to sweep out the van?" I ask. "Did you sort the treasures? Is the stroller in the back? What about your drawers? Did you put all of your laundry away? Are the LEGOs picked up? Or is there at least a path?"

Usually the answer to these questions is in the affirmative. Unfortunately, the reality may not match the answer.

This is the hard part for me, too. Often I'm not ready for inspection.

God has given me a spiritual life to keep clean and organized for Him. Most of the time mine is, at best, dusty and cluttered. There's a stray "sock" or "LEGO" I've gotten used to stepping over. I haven't checked under the sofa. I can't remember the last time I swept, mopped, or vacuumed.

I'd be hard-pressed to find anything here, like the Scriptures. Where's the Cross I'm supposed to be focusing on? Can I locate that suit of armor He gave me to wear?

What keeps me from being ready for inspection? Wrong thoughts, lies I entertain, vain imaginings. Damaged relationships, wadded up and stuffed into my dresser instead of being smoothed out. Piles of anger, bitterness, resentment, envy, and greed. All this stuff makes my path to Him almost impossible to navigate.

It's time for some serious spring cleaning. He's not threatening an inspection, just reminding me that one is coming. He wants me to make more room for His Word and less for distractions.

"Rachael? Are you ready for inspection? I'm coming back. And although I can't tell you when, I want to help you get ready. I'll give you all the wisdom and discernment you need to sort through your stuff. I'll help haul off your junk. Let's replace those things with the treasures I've chosen just for you."

A Moment of Introspection

- If you're a parent, do you inspect anything your kids have done? How does that usually turn out?
- What areas of your life are ready for inspection? What areas need some work?
- Who can you get to help you with a "spring cleaning"?

31

"Be still."

I have at least two children who are in almost constant motion. This is great when they're playing outside. It even comes in handy when I want them to wear themselves out for rest time.

There are, however, moments when sitting still would be nice—like during meals, reading, or worship. But these kids want to move then, too.

I find myself saying, "Be still" a lot! I don't want my kids to miss things because they're moving. I want them to notice important details—the sunrise, birds singing, the color of the leaves, compliments, hugs, smiles, and winks. I want them to notice changes around them, even if it means having to slow down and think so that that they don't run into something or someone.

But these kids are basically a blur. That can be frustrating when I want to look into their eyes, calmly read them a book, stroke their hair, or hold their hands. I'd like to be able to communicate with them through a smile, a glance, a gentle touch.

Maybe my kids like to keep moving because they don't want me looking into their eyes. Perhaps they're afraid of what I might see. Motion might help hide their disobedience, keep me off guard, distract me.

Recently I've become convicted about this—in reverse.

I'm starting to believe that my kids would like it if *I* sat still with *them* on occasion. I tend to be an efficiency freak, taking the saying "Idle hands are the devil's playground" literally. I like to be working on a project, dinner, sewing, writing, lesson plans, and laundry almost all the time.

I can fold laundry and teach phonics simultaneously. But my kids love it when I put it all down and do nothing except sit with them. It means everything.

There'll be a day when I can dust all I want. Now is the time for this mom to sit still with her little ones and just snuggle.

Anne Graham Lotz says that if Satan can't make you sin, he'll just keep you busy. The enemy knows the dangers to us when we're distracted—taking for granted the spectrum of colors in the fall palette, disconnecting from our children, and missing the opportunity to worship the One Who created both.

There is so much that God wants to show us, but we rush past it. We miss His soft whispers of love as He speaks through His Word and in our prayers. "Be still," He says.

Feel like things are spinning out of control, that relationships with your kids are growing shallow? Why not try a new approach, and "be still"?

A Moment of Introspection

- If you're a parent, who are your "constant motion" kids?
- How do they handle it when you ask them to "be still"?
- When was the last time you were still, doing "nothing" with your kids except being with them? What were the benefits?

32

"Where does it hurt?"

There is a thud, then loud crying, then the sound of rolling thunder as little feet rush to bring in the wounded. My daughter is covered in dirt, sweat, and blood.

"Where does it hurt?" I ask, wondering where to look to assess the damage. But she can't talk; she's too upset. I try to comfort her, telling her I love her and want to help if she will just tell me where she's hurting.

But for the moment she just wants a hug and reassurance. I guess we'll get to the source of the blood later.

When I get upset, it's much the same way. All at once I hurt everywhere and nowhere. It's everything and it's nothing. It's someone else's fault and it's all mine. "Please help me," I say, and "Please go away."

In short, I'm a real mess. Where do I hurt? All over!

Perhaps this kind of scene is repeated in heaven again and again—the thud, the consequences, the painful realities of living in a fallen world. Then there is the rush of angels' wings as they seek to help the wounded.

The angels try to get us pointed toward the throne so we can see the Great Physician. He gently asks, "Where does it hurt?"

He already knows the answer. But He asks anyway, knowing the wound is ours to identify. He knows we may choose not to reveal it. We may deny the blood flow and subsequent pain, but still He asks.

When my kids hurt, sometimes I can tell what's causing the pain—and sometimes I can't. But our heavenly Father always knows. He knows even when all we can do is stammer on and on about what happened. He knows when all we can do is cry. He knows before we are ready to admit it or when we are trying to forget.

Even though He already knows, He longs for us to pour out our hearts to Him. He wants to hear all about it, and you need not rush. He has all the time in the world. "Where does it hurt?" He asks.

Once Jesus asked a blind man, "What do you want me to do for you?" (Mark 10:51)

"What a stupid question," you might say. But some people don't want to be healed. They're perfectly content to be wounded; it's a comfortable place for them.

Are you ready to admit where you hurt? If so, it can be the first step toward healing.

A Moment of Introspection

- Where are you hurting?
- How are you dealing with your pain?
- Are you willing to trust God with your hurts?

33

> "I'm the parent, that's why."

The number one question among two-year-olds is, "Why?" It can be enough to send a young mother around the moon and back.

One day I found myself on such a lunar journey. My son had been inundating me with questions. A wise friend told me the boy was not trying to drive me crazy, but was just copying the pattern of maintaining a conversation through questions and answers.

"He is really not interested in the answer as much as imitating what he has observed, trying it out for himself," my friend explained.

Whew! For a minute I thought he'd been trying to drive me nutty! When I reflected on his questions, I realized they were truly innocent and sweet:

"Why do we put milk on our cereal?"

"Why do the birds sing?"

"Why is that man bald?"

My friend suggested I answer his questions as simply as possible. "But don't get into a pattern of trying to justify your position," she cautioned. "You are the mom, and that should be enough for him! If you realize he is challenging your authority, then he is no longer just imitating your conversation; he is trying to get you to give him a reason to obey you. And the only reason he needs to have to obey you is because you're the mom."

Unfortunately, those sweet, little "why" questions soon took a wrong turn. My son was no longer learning to maintain a conversation; he was vying for control.

"It's time to go to bed."

"Why?"

"You need to eat your vegetables."

"Why?"

"Put on your pajamas."

"Why?"

"That's enough sweets."

"Why?"

"We're not going to watch that."

"Why?"

Yep, these questions were different. He was trying to entice me into a battle of the wills.

"I'm the mom, that's why!" became my standard answer—though not an acceptable one to him.

I must admit that I'm a "why" person—even a fanatic—by nature.

I remember the day in algebra class when the teacher's assistant announced, "Remember that whatever you do to one side of the equation, you must do to the other side."

"Why?" I asked.

"That's just the way it works," she explained.

"But why?" I persisted.

"Why don't you make an appointment with me and I'll try to explain it better," she said. But she couldn't. I dropped the class—because no one could satisfy my "why" questions.

Later, during a particularly difficult time in my life, I was so focused on knowing why that I allowed it to paralyze me. The fact is that even if I'd known "why," I would not have liked it. I was using my questions as an excuse to be mad at God instead of trusting Him.

During that time I would tell God, quite angrily, "You say that You are my Father. I wouldn't treat my kids like this. And if You really loved me, You wouldn't allow me to be treated this way."

Many years later, I know His heart was breaking for me. But instead of seeing Him as caring, I was blaming Him.

I'd never dealt with my real problem—pride. I thought I knew more than everyone else. I displayed this by demanding that others prove "why" before I would participate.

My kids and I both need to learn to submit to authority, so that we'll submit to God's authority. Where He is concerned, we need to put aside our "why" demands and obey.

When we insist on understanding, we remove the need for faith and trust that He's trying to build in us. Obedience with full understanding is only common sense.

When we do what He's told us to do, without asking why, we exhibit a grasp of who He is and who we aren't. We're choosing Him over our own understanding (Proverbs 3:5-6).

God is God. He does what He pleases.
He's God, that's why.

A Moment of Introspection

- If you're a parent, how do you handle it when your kids try to manipulate or distract you with "why" questions?
- What's your number-one "why" question for God?
- Would you accept His answer, or are you using the question as an excuse?

"Stop whining!"

34

I can put up with a lot of stuff that goes with parenting, but I have no patience when it comes to whining. Along with grumbling and complaining, whining bothers me so much because it verbalizes a deeper problem—an attitude of ingratitude.

Whining usually is accompanied by rash, ridiculous, selfish, shallow statements:

"No one understands me!"

"I'm bored!"

"I never get to do that!"

A lack of thankfulness for the basic blessing of life is a setup for great disappointment. A person with that outlook feels there are more things to complain about than to celebrate. To him or her the glass is not only half empty, it's also dirty and broken.

Eeyore, that *Winnie-the-Pooh* donkey, comes to mind. He's a cute cartoon character, in a pathetic kind of way. But he's so sad and gloomy, going around with a cloud over his head. I can hear him talking in that depressing tone of voice: "We're nevvvver gonnnna make it."

I have a favorite scripture for whining kids. Philippians 2:14

says we're to do everything "without complaining or arguing." At our house we've added "yelling and screaming" on occasion.

I realize some parents don't see it this way. They consider whining to be cute, a rite of passage, a necessary evil, a passing phase. But entertaining, tolerating, or giving in to this behavior tends to establish it as a pattern or habit.

The same is true with us adults. In fact, the things our kids whine to us about tend to be the things we whine to God about.

"You never did that for me!"

"You wouldn't have let this happen if You really loved me!"

"I had it first!"

"She looked at me funny!"

Whining causes the hairs on the back of my neck to stand on end. I'm not suggesting that God has the same response, but I'm sure He's hurt and disappointed. He's hurt because we've doubted Him, His abilities, and His concern. He's disappointed that we allow anything in creation to eclipse the Creator.

When we whine, we need to consider where we're looking. Which way are we facing? Are we no longer facing Him?

God wants us to consider all His provisions, to count our many blessings. No matter how bad things are, He is still God. He cares, and is able to sustain us in our darkest hour.

I love what Job says when all seems lost: "The LORD gave and the LORD has taken away; may the name of the LORD be praised" (Job 1:21b). And then later, "Though he slay me, yet will I hope in him" (13:15a).

Job, a man with every reason to whine, was not focused on his own circumstance but on a holy, awesome, mighty God. Job was not looking down at the mud, but staring at the Maker of the stars.

Job's glass was not half empty, but filled to overflowing. He was grateful, clear on who he was—and who God is.

Moment of Introspection

- If you're a parent, how do you handle it when your kids whine?
- What are you most disgruntled about? Do you whine out loud about it, or just to yourself?
- When was the last time you counted your blessings? Could you do that today?

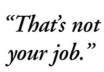

35

"That's not your job."

As the next to the youngest of our seven kids, Joseph was bound to have more than one mom. There's always someone ready, if not anxious, to tell him what to do.

"Stop that, Joseph."

"Say 'please,' Joseph."

"Put that away, Joseph."

"Sit down, Joseph."

"No, Joseph."

Sometimes it must be tough to be Joseph, with so many voices coming at him.

What Joseph needs most from his brothers and sisters is not another command, but encouragement and blessing. I believe the correction, reproof, and discipline are for Davis and me to do.

The other day this conflict of roles came to a predictable head. The kids were playing when Joseph accidentally hit his little brother on the head with a toy car.

Assuming the mommy role, Molly took Joseph's hand and gently smacked it. "No," she said firmly, looking him in the eyes.

Molly will make a great mom someday. But until then, that's not her job.

I told her that. Then I added, "Your job is to love and bless your brother, not correct or train him."

Molly already knew it wasn't her job; we'd been over that many times. But she couldn't resist the urge to do it anyway. It felt so nice to be the smacker and not the smackee.

Why do kids so enjoy correcting each other? Why is it easier to boss than to bless?

Certainly it's more fun to arrest than to be arrested, more fun to discipline than to be disciplined. But kids also use sibling policing as a diversionary tactic. Instead of doing what they've been asked to do, they draw attention to another child's failings.

It's easy to get sidetracked as a parent, too. Some things are not my job.

It's my job to encourage my kids, to point them in the way they should go. It's my job to accept them, listen to them, equip them, and train them for God's glory. But sometimes I overstep my bounds.

It's not my job to convict them. That's His job.

I can't really empower them, either. That's His job.

It's not my job to grow spiritually on their behalf, though I'm responsible to provide a safe, nurturing, encouraging environment in which He can help them grow.

I must resist the urge to take on tasks that are not my job. I'll fail at them, because I'm working in my strength and not His, for my own agenda and not His will.

The number one thing I want for my kids is that God

would be real to them—not a far-off-in-heaven God, or an impersonal "take a number" God, or a thunder and lightning God. But I can't make them believe in or embrace Him. Yet I can hold Him up before them, point them to Him every day, seek Him on their behalf. I can live my faith in front of them. That is my joy and my job.

Sometimes I find myself in the middle of a project that I took on without prayer; I raised my hand at some meeting and volunteered rashly. As a result, the things I need to do are suffering because I'm doing someone else's job.

It's easy for God to see those times in advance. "Please let Me do that for you, Rachael," He says. "That is not your job. There are so many other things I need you to be doing. When you take on jobs that aren't yours, you miss out on seeing Me work."

That's why I need to be careful to do only the things He's assigned me to do.

A Moment of Introspection

- If you're a parent, do your children take on jobs that aren't theirs? If so, what happens?
- When you take on someone else's job, what's the result?
- Are there some jobs you've taken on that are actually God's? How can you avoid doing this in the future?

36

"*[Your name here]*"

" **C** harles!"
    "Anderson!"
  "Savannah Anne!"
  "Molly!"
  "Elizabeth!"
  "Joseph!"
  "Benjamin!"
  A bunch of name-calling goes on at our house.

I'll be the first to admit, though, that I don't always call the name I'm intending. I've even been known to use extended family names as well as those of good friends and their children.

As a last resort, I've been known to say, "Whoever I am looking at, I am talking to you!" Obviously this response is not always workable, since the person I'm trying to call may not be in front of me. We often just choose to laugh at these moments.

But sometimes it's not funny that mom can't say the right name. It's not funny to me or to the child.

I want to remember the right name so the child knows that I know who he or she is. I want the child to be sure that I realize he or she is a unique person, created by God to fulfill His specific plan.

When I forget a child's name, I can sometimes see an uncertain and even unforgiving look in his or her eyes. For a moment I can hear that unspoken question: "Does she really know who she's talking to? Does she have me confused with someone else?" All I can do is apologize and pray to do better.

In this fallen world, my mind is cluttered with the unimportant. Its ability to remember important things—like my kids' names—is inhibited.

But God doesn't have that problem. He never calls me by someone else's name. When He calls, He is never distracted by His other children or the goings-on throughout the universe. He never says, "Whoever you are, I am talking to you!"

He is the Almighty One who created me in my mother's womb. He saw me before anyone else did. He knows me more intimately than anyone else does. And He calls me by my name every time.

I know that He loves me, and that He wants what's best for me. When I hear Him call my name, I can be sure He has something wise to share with me. He wants to remind me of who He is, or tell me about His plan for my life, or encourage me in my struggles, or warn me of danger.

There is nothing like the sound of Him calling my name. My goal is to listen and answer in anticipation of His truth.

A Moment of Introspection

- If you're a parent, do you ever get your kids' names confused? How do they respond?
- Do you believe God knows your name? Why or why not?
- If God is calling your name, what do you think He wants to tell you?

37

> ## "Use your time wisely."

T ime management is a skill some adults never master. Most children don't, either.

I want my kids to improve in this area, of course. I don't want to have to keep telling them what needs to be done next, and when. In other words, I want them to skip the learning period called childhood and slide into responsible adulthood.

Yeah, right.

With seven kids, do I have time to teach them all time management? I keep trying. For example, there was that experiment I undertook with our two boys.

"This Friday your dad and I are going on a date," I announced. "I am betting that you are going to want to watch a movie while we are gone. Whether you do or not will depend on if you use your time wisely this week and complete your assignment sheet."

Five days stretched out before us—endless time, it seemed. I cautioned the boys to allow a good margin of flexibility for unpredictable events life might throw at us. I even tossed in Ben

Franklin's famous quote, "Don't put off until tomorrow what you can do today."

They didn't know I had set them up. I was trying to figure out how they worked best. Their assignment sheets were legitimate, as was our week's schedule, but I had a broader agenda.

One of the boys went right to work; he appreciates a list. He made good progress until a person got in his way. Since "Be kind to your sister" didn't make the checklist, he finished the day's assignments but missed several opportunities to build relationships.

My other son adopted a "later" mentality. The assignment sheet could wait; a week was a long time. By the end of the day he had several projects at various stages of completion, but none finished. He did, however, include his sisters in his assignments. He ended the day with nothing marked off his list, but at peace.

I learned a lot about the boys that week, things that have helped me as their mother and teacher. But I also learned a lot about me.

Some of the things I already knew—like the fact that I love a list. But I discovered that I, too, often view people as an interruption instead of an opportunity. I learned that at the age of 38 I still have not mastered real time management.

"Use your time wisely, Rachael," I believe I can sometimes hear God say. He may almost whisper it in my ear when I'm irritated by a friend, neighbor, or one of my kids.

What is the wisest use of time? When I'm in the middle of being productive, it may mean stopping for the child who wants to show me the wildflower she picked just for me or the picture

she drew. It may mean ignoring the dirty dishes in the sink, the
piles of laundry on the floor, and the dust accumulating on every
surface in order to take a walk with the kids.

It may mean getting up early to start the day in the Word
and on my knees. It may mean meeting with a friend to pray for
our families, or stepping outside my comfort zone to meet the
needs of others.

All of these are examples of using my time wisely, though
none would make my narrow to-do list for most days.

"Use your time wisely."

It's as though He whispers it in the morning when He wants
to take a walk and I want to stay in bed. I seem to hear it, too,
when I reach for the TV remote or the telephone to escape from
a frustrating or tiring day.

"Use your time wisely. Seek Me, talk to Me, serve Me, wait
on Me. Time with Me is never wasted. Your list is not going any-
where."

A Moment of Introspection

- If you're a parent, what are some "time wasters" that
  tempt your children?
- Do you tend to waste time, or waste opportunities
  to build relationships?
- How could it make a difference in the Kingdom if
  you choose to use your time more wisely?

38

> "I love to hear
> you sing."

"Low in the gravy lay, Jesus my Savior . . ."

Growing up, I used to sing this hymn and imagine Jesus lying in gravy, wondering what that had to do with anything. Being from the South, where gravy is part of any good main course instead of just a sauce, I thought it made even less sense. But who was I to question the Lord?

Another song I routinely messed up was the one that helped us learn the books of the New Testament. Right after Philemon, I thought, the song said, "He bruised James." For most of my childhood I thought it unfortunate that Philemon had caused this injury. Later I discovered "he bruised" was "Hebrews."

In keeping with this family tradition, my kids have come up with some pretty funny renditions of the old favorites. But no matter the words, it's their hearts that are beautiful when I hear them singing as they play, color, clean, or bathe. There's something so sweet and innocent in their voices, so tender, so sincere. When I catch them singing, I sometimes giggle to myself—and sometimes am overwhelmed at their bold proclamations.

I suspect they often don't know the meaning of phrases like

"nothing but the blood of Jesus" and "Be Thou my vision, oh Lord of my heart." The tunes have hooked them.

They may not get it, but I do. And someday they will, too.

I'm convinced that the God of the universe loves to hear me sing, too. The Lord wanted His people to sing to Him in the days of old (Jeremiah 31:7), and encourages us to keep singing today (Ephesians 5:19).

When I sing He pauses, I believe, to lean in closer. He smiles as I struggle with the melody or the lyrics. He sheds a tear as I choke back my own, when I begin to learn the real meaning of the words.

These are the old hymns I learned sitting on the left side of the sanctuary, second pew, next to my mother every Sunday morning. These hymns, whose truths I've come to learn through my own personal experience, He loves to hear me sing.

"Count your many blessings, name them one by one . . ."

"Angry words, oh let them never from the tongue unbridled slip . . ."

"When peace like a river attendeth my way . . ."

"A mighty fortress is our God, a bulwark never failing . . ."

Knowing hymns and praise songs has ministered to my heart and soul. In the tough times, when I've felt alone, misunderstood, rejected, hurt, frustrated, overwhelmed, and even hopeless, singing to my heavenly Father has meant the most to me.

At one such time, when I felt trapped, isolated, and discouraged, I spent many days just crying. Finally a concerned friend suggested I get some praise music going: "You can't change the situation, but you have got to change your attitude. And the best way I know to do that is to get the focus off of you and get it onto Him. Get yourself some tapes and start singing again!"

I did, halfheartedly at first. Then I heard a new song, one that seemed to have been written just for me: "God will make a way where there seems to be no way . . ."

There was a way for me! That became my theme song. I sang it often when I wanted to do something stupid, when I wanted to give up. He showed me the way, and I sang all the way there!

It stirs the heart of the King of heaven when one of His children sings to Him—even when the song is as simple as, "Jesus loves me, this I know, for the Bible tells me so."

A Moment of Introspection

- If you're a parent, what are some songs your kids sing?
- What does your singing reveal about your heart?
- What hymn or praise song is your favorite? How could singing it now influence the rest of your day?

39

*"Don't lie
to me."*

As a child, I was a serial liar.

And I was good at it.

I lied about hiding my black patent leather Sunday shoes, cleaning my room, buying candy—anything I didn't want to tell the truth about. And my mother believed me.

Now, as a mom myself, I don't want my kids to suffer the consequences of habitual lying. That's why I find myself having conversations like the following.

"Okay, who spilled the orange juice?"

"Not me!"

"Not me!"

"Not me!"

"I know one of you did. Who was it?"

"Not me!"

"Not me!"

"Not me!"

Great, I think.

"Okay," I say out loud. "You three sit here and figure it out together. And when you all figure it out, come and tell me. We cannot get on with the day until we get to the bottom of this. I will set the timer, and if it goes off before you have it settled, you will all pay the price together."

They stare blankly at each other for a couple of minutes before negotiations begin.

It's interesting to watch what happens. The culprit almost visibly weighs the options. He or she wants to check all the side doors before going out the front.

The innocent, meanwhile, try to piece the truth together. They listen to the timer . . . *tick, tick, tick.* They think, *I didn't do anything. How did I get here? I don't want to go down for something I didn't do. Man, who did it?*

Personal responsibility. It's a great thing when there are accolades to be collected and admiration to relish; but with guilt and punishment waiting in the wings, it's repulsive to consider. It's like cod liver oil: "Who said it was good for me? I beg to differ. I'm willing to skip the long-term benefits if I can skip the short-term taste."

Truth-telling is important. I want to teach my kids the importance of taking personal responsibility. I want them to forsake selfish blame-shifting and to stand by their actions. That's why I say to them, "I want you to tell me the truth."

It's pathetic to see a child whose hands are paint-covered and hear him deny that he touched the paint. The excuses are laughable: "Someone pushed me." "I tripped." "I was trying to keep someone else from touching the wall." "I noticed a fly on the wall and was trying to take it off."

How about the truth? How about confirming the obvious?

How about humbly admitting the action? What a breath of fresh air that would be!

And then there's me.

At times God brings something to my mind, gently prodding me to be truthful about a person or situation: "Rachael, I want you to tell Me the truth." Almost immediately I try to deny it on a technicality, push the blame onto someone else, or flat-out lie.

"I haven't forgiven them because they didn't ask me for forgiveness," I say.

"I didn't take a meal because I didn't know they needed one."

"I wasn't gossiping—I was asking for prayer on their behalf."

"I would have prayed, but they don't like me."

My excuses must make Him very sad. "Don't lie to Me," He urges.

I know what the truthful answers would be. They would reveal ugliness, selfishness, so unlike what He wants my attitude to be toward others. Telling the truth would mean humbling myself, letting Him work through me to extend His forgiveness, love, and grace. My lies keep me enslaved; the truth waits to set me free to experience the abundant life He's promised.

When my kids sit there with the timer, "working it out" together, the truth usually emerges. The innocent breathe a sigh of relief. They're grateful that the culprit will take the fall without them.

They also learn a valuable lesson. Contrary to popular belief, lying is not something that can be done without affecting others. It's not without its victims.

The psalmist writes, "Surely you desire truth in the inner parts" (Psalm 51:6). Like my kids, I must speak the truth, take responsibility for my actions, and seek to glorify God in all things.

A Moment of Introspection

- If you're a parent, when was the last time your kids lied to you? How did you respond?
- When was the last time you lied? Why and to whom did you lie?
- How might telling the truth "set you free"?

40

"Pay attention."

This might be the number one thing I say to my kids.

Naturally, that means I, too, often sense God saying things like this to me:

"Hello?"

"What are you thinking?"

"Pay attention!"

"Is there anybody in there?"

"Where are you?"

"Get with the program!"

"Snap out of it!"

"Earth to Rachael. Come in, Rachael."

But let's get back to my kids. Sometimes they have the "lights are on, but no one is home" look. You know the one I mean. They're looking right at me, yet they're a million miles away. They might manage to give me a correct answer, but they're not with the program.

Case in point: One day at Wal-Mart. Or Wally World, as we affectionately call it.

I often find a wealth of learning opportunities at Wally

World. It's fun when you can glean from others, though, instead of being the main attraction.

On this particular day our number must have been up; we were center ring. Our time in the spotlight was like a clown act where everything goes wrong. It was a comedy of errors without the laughter.

Our miserable day started in the parking lot when we discovered that we'd forgotten Joseph's blanket and sippy cup. These should have been a sign of things to come, but we ignored them and went on.

Inside the store I was going to drop off prescriptions, but didn't have my prescription card. *I'll just drop them off and pick them up later,* I thought.

Things went from bad to worse. There was a dirty diaper without any wipes; an accidental wetting of training pants with no backup; yogurt dropped in the dairy section resulting in a "Wet cleanup on Aisle Two"; and a busted lip during a wrestling match over a free cookie.

Somewhere in the store I lost my list, which probably symbolized my brain. When the total was finalized, I was short of cash.

It was a terrible, horrible, no good, very bad day.

I wanted to blame the kids. After all, they'd been darting in different directions, asking for things they knew I wouldn't buy. They'd been arguing about who could touch the cart. Now they were tired, sweating, crying, and bleeding.

If they'd just been paying attention, none of this would have happened!

Okay, *I* was the one who hadn't been paying attention. I'd forgotten to check the diaper bag for wipes and extra training pants. I'd meant to get a sippy cup, but had been distracted. I'd known cookies were going to be an issue, and the predictable fight had ensued. I'd lost my list and hadn't brought enough money.

At the end of the day the only thing I couldn't take the blame for was the yogurt mess. And guess what I'd said when that occurred? "If you would just pay attention, things like that wouldn't happen."

Things *would* go better if only I'd pay attention.

If only I'd pay attention to God's will instead of mine.

If only I'd pay attention to the opportunities He places right in front of me instead of going out of my way to do what I want.

Often I get to the end of a day of not paying attention, wanting to blame the comedy of errors on someone else. "They weren't paying attention to me," I complain.

Then it's as though I hear Him say, "Pay attention to *you*? Why don't you try paying attention to *Me*?

"I promise that if you'll pay attention to Me and the plans I have for your life, you'll find things go well for you. You've tried paying attention to everything else. Why not Me?"

A Moment of Introspection

- If you're a parent, when do you most need your kids to pay attention to you?
- Who and what are you paying attention to?
- Who and what do you need to focus on more?

"*Call home.*"

41

My mother used to say this to me. She always wanted me to call when I arrived at the destination. But she also wanted me to call if something went wrong.

My generation wasn't the "mobile phone on everyone's hip" generation. I was part of the "25 cents a call on the pay phone" generation. Making a call home took effort and was easily forgotten or put off indefinitely. And Mom couldn't call me to check on how I was doing.

"If you're going to be late, call home," she'd say.

"If you miss your ride, call home."

"If you change your mind, call home."

"If you need anything, call home."

Many times I forgot to call home when I was supposed to. Many times Mom told me how she'd worried because I hadn't called. She'd remind me how important it was to call, and I'd promise to do better.

As I face the prospect of children learning to drive and taking jobs and running errands, I anticipate saying "Call home" a lot. Why? Because I want them to know I'm here for whatever they might need.

I'd also love it if they'd call home just to say "Hey" and tell me how their evening is going. Maybe they could even slip in an "I love you" or "See you later." I want them to call me just *because*—because I matter to them, because they know I care about them, because they enjoy sharing their lives with me. That would affirm our relationship.

God wants me to call home, too. He calls it prayer. It's the desire of His heart to have a personal relationship with me.

He's there when I have emergencies and other needs, of course. But He also wants to be there in my moment-by-moment thoughts and experiences. He wants us to have an ongoing relationship that includes an ongoing conversation.

If I'm hurting, He wants me to call home.

If I'm lonely, He wants me to call home.

If I'm angry, He wants me to call home.

If I'm excited, He wants me to call home.

If I'm confused, He wants me to call home.

For any and every reason, He wants me to call home—to call on His name and tell Him all about it. Calling home isn't for His benefit, but for mine—though it brings Him great pleasure to hear from His children.

I don't know about you, but I fear being lost. When I was first learning to drive I loved to go for a quick spin. But a couple of times I got lost—really lost. To make matters worse, it was dark—and Mom and Dad were out for the evening. It was before cell phones; I just kept driving until I figured things out through my tears and panic.

Oh, I wish I could have called home! I would have loved to hear Daddy's voice say, "Kitten, are you okay? Where are you? Sit tight, I'll come and get you." Oh, the relief—just to know my daddy knew and that he cared and was on the way.

Spiritually speaking, I still like to take a ride all by myself sometimes. I strike out on my own in no particular direction, as night falls. Soon I find myself surrounded by unfamiliar places and strange faces.

God is the ultimate OnStar operator. He watches and patiently waits.

All I have to do is call home. Before I know it, He's there to show me the way back, to make my path straight, to take me into His arms.

A Moment of Introspection

- If you're a parent, have your kids ever called you "just because"? If so, how did that make you feel?
- When have you "called" your heavenly Father? What was the reason?
- Have you "called" recently just to tell Him you love Him? Could you do so today?

42

> *"Let me know*
> *when you*
> *get some*
> *self-control."*

I had a great first pediatrician when the boys were very young. I can still hear Dr. Elberson telling me that the way to know when to bring in a child with a bad rash was when the child was more uncomfortable than I was.

He gave me advice for picky eaters, too: three squares a day without snacks. "They will eventually get hungry enough to eat good, nutritious food," he said. He was right.

The doctor also had some great counsel on tantrums: "Ignore them whenever possible. Make sure the child is safe and unlikely to hurt himself, but do not pay attention to the behavior. Let the child know that when they are ready to talk you are available, but that you will not respond to inappropriate behavior."

When my first son was born, I was one day away from being 24 years old. That wasn't incredibly young, but I was incredibly naive. How could such a cute, cuddly, little person be so manipulative? Where did he learn it? It seemed to be hardwired into him.

I was so green as a mom that when Charles threw his first

fit at 18 months, I thought it meant we were going to get the "terrible twos" over early. (I must say here that I no longer believe in the "terrible twos" or the "dreaded teenage years," as these generalities twist our expectations about some important periods in our children's development.)

Now to the story. Charles and I were at the grocery store, just the two of us. He pointed to something he wanted; I said a firm "No." That's when it all started.

The "No" turned out to be a trigger. He began screaming and yelling, going on and on. You'd think he had stepped on a nail.

It got so bad that I did something I'd never done before and haven't done since: I left a half-filled shopping cart at the store and drove away.

By the time we got home, Charles was still screaming. He hadn't let up the whole way. Thinking something might be wrong, I checked him for bites and cuts, but there were none.

I called Davis. "What is going on?" he asked.

"I said 'no' at the grocery store, and he has not let up," I replied.

Ironically, the doctor and I had discussed this subject just the week before. During a well visit, the pediatrician had asked whether Charles had thrown any tantrums.

"No," I'd proudly replied, thinking tantrums were a symptom of bad parenting. Now, standing in my kitchen 30 minutes after turning down Charles' request, watching the boy roll on the floor, screaming, I had a different perspective. I was overwhelmed by the ugliness of his fit as well as its futility.

As gently as I could, I picked him up and carried him to his room for a nap. He screamed a little more—then took a very long, hard rest.

When he got up, I talked to him about his yelling. It was not an appropriate way to respond to me or his daddy, I said.

It was a speech I've had the opportunity to give many times over.

As Charles grew older and other siblings tried out similar behavior, I would say in the middle of the tantrum, "Let me know when you have some self-control, so that we can talk."

Tantrums are ugly things, uncontrolled fits of rage and selfishness. And the only thing uglier than a tantrum at two is a tantrum at thirty-eight!

I'm too sophisticated to throw myself on the floor anymore. But my screams, though silent, would rival my two-year-old's if they could be heard. I'm able to hide my defiance behind a façade of cooperation and smiles; my manipulative tactics may have matured with age, but they're no less selfish.

Just as my sweet, blonde-haired, blue-eyed, little buddy could turn into a red-faced, teary-eyed bundle of frustration, I sometimes regress into a tantrum. These fits can occur at any time, but especially when I'm told "No"—or whenever things don't work out the way I want them to.

Who am I kidding? Do I really think my heavenly Father doesn't see my tantrums? He sees. He sees me cross my arms, closing off my heart to His touch. He hears my silent "No!" Just because I have everyone else fooled, it doesn't mean He is. He shakes His head and says, "Oh, My child."

I should know better. And maybe someday I will, when I've heard that soundbite from heaven often enough: "Let Me know when you have some self-control, so that we can talk."

A Moment of Introspection

- If you're a parent, do your kids have tantrums? If so, how do you respond?
- Are you seeking to teach your child self-control? How?
- Is there any issue about which you're throwing a mental tantrum these days? If so, what's one thing you can do to develop more self-control?

"*Be quiet!*"

43

A h, silence.

It's something I have to pursue to experience. It's something I appreciate more than I thought possible. It's a valuable context in which to contemplate the things of life, and something I want more of.

That's why I like early morning. I can get up before the sounds of the day start and have some time to organize my thoughts before there's too much competition for clarity. I can think about God's faithfulness and allow peace, contentment, joy, hope, love, and patience to wash over me and fill me for the day ahead.

Of course, not every morning starts out that way. Welcome to Carman Central.

It's still dark when she enters our bedroom. "Daddy, I had an accident," she announces.

Davis walks her to our bathroom while I find the light. *It's 4:30 A.M.,* I think. *How does she do that?* Those other 30 minutes really would have been nice.

We clean her up and get her back to her room.

At 7:00 A.M. Davis calls the boys to get moving. The silence is gone.

"Make your bed."

"What is the plan for the day?"

"The bed is wet."

"Brush your hair."

"Are we going to the store?"

"I can't find my sandals."

"She won't help me."

"Benjamin is crying."

"Something stinks."

"I didn't sleep good last night."

"There's something in my eye."

"Turn the radio off."

"What day is it?"

"I don't have any clean underwear."

"We're out of cereal."

"The toilet is clogged."

"Has anyone fed the fish yet?"

Disappearing silence is not just a morning phenomenon at our house. It happens at nap time, too.

I don't usually get to indulge in a nap, but on this particular day I was especially tired. After getting the kids separated, the phones turned off, and the baby nursed, I laid myself down. *Oh,* I thought, *this is going to be really nice.*

I'd started the dishwasher to provide a soothing background hum. We were all drifting off when I began to hear a different sound—a foot tapping.

(Important note: Since I've had children, my hearing has drastically improved. Mom says that I used to be able to sleep through anything; now the slightest noise or vibration can interrupt my sleep. I can hear a baby roll over down the hall, or a pacifier drop to the floor. Incredible, yes—but also inhibiting.)

Back to my nap. At the sound of the tapping foot, I said without opening my eyes, "Be quiet."

"Yes, Ma'am," came the response.

I dozed, only to be roused by another sound—the tossing of a Beanie Baby.

Sitting up, I said, "Be quiet! Please let me rest."

Again I began to doze. You guessed it: Another new sound kept me from being able to nap. This time I not only sat up and opened my eyes, I got up and stood over the culprit. "This is not quiet," I announced. "I have asked you to do a simple thing, but you have chosen disobedience."

You might think that as a maker of such divine-sounding pronouncements, I would remember the value God places on silence. But sometimes I don't.

Too often I go to Him with a noisy rush of questions and complaints:

"Why did this have to happen?"

"Would You please fix this situation?"

"How can I do this?"

"I wish You would do such and such."

Psalm 46:10 says, "Be still, and know that I am God." To "be still and know" is to take in His Creation, to contemplate the wonders of His hands, consider His ways, meditate on His laws.

During stillness and silence I have the opportunity to embrace His glory and goodness. The list of things I want Him to do fades in comparison to who He is. My focus changes from what He can do for me to who He is—from His hands to His shining face.

There is great peace in being quiet.

A Moment of Introspection

- If you're a parent, what do you try to teach your kids about being quiet?
- Do you take time to be quiet before the Lord? If so, when?
- Keeping in mind Psalm 46:10, how "quiet" are your quiet times before Him?

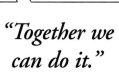

"Together we
can do it."

44

"I can't!"
I hate to hear my kids say this.

Rarely does the phrase mean what it seems to. When they
say it, my children usually don't mean that they're unable. They
mean they don't want to, that it's too hard, or that they're too
tired. Sometimes they say it for attention, as a distraction, or out
of frustration.

Even when they really can't, crying "I can't!" isn't acceptable.
They're surrounded by people who love them, and "Together we
can!"

Davis and I encourage our kids to replace "I can't!" with
"Help!"

But that's not easy—not only for them, but also for me. I
don't want to admit that I need help, that alone I really can't. It's
humiliating; it makes me feel vulnerable.

I can figure it out, I think. *I've got it, really. After all, I have a
college degree. How hard can anything be? If I just try harder, I can
do it all by myself.*

"Be all you can be!" "You can do anything you put your

mind to!" "Believe you can, and you will!" These statements reflect our individualistic culture. "We" has been reduced to "I."

I've prided myself on my independence, competence, and self-sufficiency. But God created me for relationships—to need Him and others.

Long before I did, God knew that I "couldn't." That's been His plan all along. Still, I insist on trying to do it all by myself, just as my kids do.

I must look pretty silly to the Master as I struggle to accomplish something He wants me to do—but never intended for me to do alone. He wants us to do it *together*, so I can get to know Him better, so I can realize how much He loves me, so I can experience His love and grace.

The point is not for me to prove something, to add to my list of accomplishments. He wants me to enjoy working with Him, doing His will, His way.

It's like those times when two-year-old Joseph wants to button his shirt. Excited about doing it himself, he focuses on the task. But quickly he gets frustrated; the little buttons are so hard to hold with his pudgy little fingers, and the holes are so small. He tries and tries, but they just won't fit together.

He yells, grunts, groans, spins around, pulls at the shirt, kicks the air. He refuses help, insisting, "Me do!"

Tears finally fall, and he sits down in surrender. He still doesn't want help. He wants another shirt—one without buttons!

For me, the challenge hasn't been shirts; it's been seven children. I didn't want a really big family in the beginning; in fact, we even thought about never having kids! That's funny to reflect on now that we're greatly blessed with four boys and three girls. If I've heard it once, I've heard it a million times: "I don't know how you do it!"

My response takes people by surprise: "I don't."

The most important thing I've learned by being the mother of seven is that "I can't." I can't be supremely patient, amazingly organized, and meet each child's needs. I can't do all the things most people assume I can since I have all these children.

Realizing my inadequacies has been both humbling and liberating. It's taught me that I'll fail apart from Him and those He's sent to help me. Together we always succeed.

Still, I sometimes push Him away, or push away those He's sent. *It looks easy enough*, I think. *I can handle this one.*

Soon I find myself flustered, irritated, working myself into a lather. Eventually I give up. Instead of asking for help, I ask for a change of venue. I want to try something else. I didn't like that shirt anyway.

If only I would remember that "together we can do it."

A Moment of Introspection

- When has your whole family worked together on a project? How did it turn out?
- Is there something you're trying to do the hard way, alone? Why?
- What kind of help do you need? At what point might you be willing to ask for it?

45

"Please just trust and obey me."

Immediate, unquestioning, cheerful obedience is a beautiful thing.

And oh, so rare.

Often I need that kind of obedience because I don't have the time, desire, or words to explain why. I just need them to do what I've asked because I've proven myself trustworthy. They should know I wouldn't ask if it weren't important.

After all, I'm the parent. I know things my kids don't know, things they can't understand.

Davis and I learned at a conference to practice this kind of obedience with our kids to prepare them for times when compliance would be crucial. We've asked them to go get things or even stand on their heads. It may sound silly, but it's an effort to teach them the important skill of trusting and obeying.

We've been grateful to have practiced this kind of obedience. On one of our cross-country trips, for example, we were running low on gas. We ended up in one of those way-off-the-beaten-path joints. It looked okay on the outside as Davis was pumping gas, but when we went in to eat, the crew inside looked pretty shady.

The kids didn't notice any of this. "Cool!" they were saying. "Pizza, tacos, or chicken!"

We sat down, Davis and I exchanging glances of concern. Our family was too large to sit at one table. I had my back to a couple who seemed to be watching us from the moment we walked in the door. Their conversation was making me very uncomfortable.

When our girls headed for the restroom, one of the people from the other table followed. I went, too. On my return it seemed clear that we had to leave—now.

Davis told the kids, "I need you to do what I am about to ask you to do the first time without question, just like we practice at home. I know that you are not finished eating, but we are leaving. Please get up and follow me to the car."

The preparation paid off. We made it to the car without incident—and without whining. Once we were in the car, the questions came quickly—as did our thanks for the kids' obedience.

God wants me and you to trust and obey without question, hesitation, grumbling, or stalling. He wants us to trust Him enough to simply act.

I don't always do that, of course. Sometimes I put off obeying, hoping God won't notice or that He'll change His mind.

For instance, there was a time when a friend gave me credit I didn't deserve. She went on and on thanking me, and I didn't correct her. I accepted her accolades and soaked it all in, knowing it was wrong and that the credit belonged to someone else. The Holy Spirit kept prompting me to admit what I'd done, and I kept ignoring Him. Finally, after one too many sleepless nights,

I explained the whole thing to my friend; it was embarrassing, but necessary. What *wasn't* necessary was my delay in obeying.

That's also true when God asks me to do something that seems downright odd or uncomfortable. At those times He tests my trust and love for Him.

Faith is believing in what you can't see. I can't see the future or His plan for my life; I can't see how my disobedience affects the picture He's painting. What He asks me to do may seem ridiculous, but that shouldn't matter.

All that should matter is this: Do I trust Him enough to obey Him, especially when it doesn't seem to make sense?

Like my kids, I need to just trust and obey.

A Moment of Introspection

- If you're a parent, how might your kids be blessed if they'd just trust and obey you?
- What are you waiting to understand before you trust and obey?
- How has God shown you that He's trustworthy? How has that affected your willingness to obey Him?

46

"Listen to me."

66 Charles, I want you to go out to the garage and get me a roll of paper towels."

He comes back with a hammer.

"Get your instruments in the car."

We arrive at music lessons with nothing to play.

My kids actually did listen to me, at least once. Here's how it happened.

Pregnant with Joseph, I wearily started cooking dinner. Elizabeth was napping; the older four were playing chase in the front yard. I'd just checked on them through the front window.

All was peaceful—until Anderson burst through the back door. "Savannah Anne fell! She's bleeding bad! Charles is bringing her in."

I remained calm; blood didn't scare me.

Charles entered, shoulder covered in blood, carrying his sister. Even before I saw the cut, it didn't look good. When I was able to manage a peek, I could see she needed stitches.

"Okay, listen to me," I ordered. "Savannah Anne, you remain calm. We are going to the emergency room. Anderson, you get her to the van and buckled up. Then come back and get the diaper bag. Charles, you go and wake Elizabeth up and get on her socks and shoes. Then take her to the van and buckle her up. Molly, you go on to the van now and stay with Savannah Anne while the rest of us get everything else together to go."

Immediately we charged in different directions. I grabbed my purse, turned off dinner, and found additional gauze for the wound. We were out of the house in under five minutes.

And we had everything, all because they listened to me.

At other times, things have not gone so well. I've talked, chided, rebuked, corrected, and gone on and on, only to be totally tuned out. Sometimes this happens when my kids are looking me right in the eye, which is concerning. I may as well be speaking a different language.

Sometimes it's a case of defiantly tuning me out. It's a haughty determination not to listen, a lack of humility and submission to authority.

At other times it's a case of thinking they know more than I do. This even happens when they come to me with questions: "Where is my dress?" "How do I make this cake?" "When should I call?" They ask for my input, but don't listen to it. They may even return later to ask why their course of action didn't work.

Yet sometimes they truly hear me. At these times they're really searching for an answer and listen with all their hearts. Those are teachable moments, the kind parents should relish.

"Listen, my son," wrote Solomon (Proverbs 1:8). In these words, you can hear a father's longing. He's pleading with his son to learn from a father's triumphs and mistakes. I greatly appreciate

Proverbs not only for its depth of wisdom, but also because it reflects a parent's fervent attempt to train his son.

The whole Bible holds our heavenly Father's love story for each of us. He wants us to listen to His wisdom, really listen. His Word says we will find Him when we seek Him with all our hearts.

It's hard to listen when you're talking, and I've found that I talk too much. Often it's because I'm trying to hide my sin with many words. Or I'm trying to talk God into giving me an answer I want. If I'm fooling anyone, it's only me.

I don't have all the answers for my kids, but God does. I imagine He is often saying, "Rachael, listen to Me."

To do that, I have to spend time in His Word, seeking His truth. I have to be quiet. I have to open my ears and close my mouth.

That kind of listening takes work. But if we really want to hear from God, we will.

A Moment of Introspection

- If you're a parent, when are your kids most open to hearing what you have to say?
- When are you most interested in listening to God? Why?
- How have you used "teachable moments" with your kids? How has God used them with you?

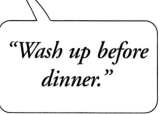

47

"*Wash up before dinner.*"

The boys started early that summer morning, gathering buckets, nets, and peanut butter jars. They were out the door right after breakfast, headed for a boys' dream day full of tadpoles and frogs, turtles and caterpillars, salamanders and mudpuppies—not to mention mud, mosquitoes, and general messiness.

They were gone for a couple of hours in the vastness of our backyard, down at the creek, climbing trees, chasing through the woods. They didn't know I could see them from the window; our one-acre lot seemed so big to them, they were lost in it.

When they came in for dinner, they were dirty. Those hands had been a million places—in the creek, the tree trunks, and the mud. They bore traces of slime, dirt, poop, and miscellaneous gook.

Those hands were screaming for about a gallon of antibacterial soap and some really hot water. But it didn't occur to the boys to rinse, much less scrub.

"Go and wash up before dinner," I said.

"They are not that dirty, Mom," came the reply.

"Go wash up!"

"Yes, Ma'am."

They returned, having only rinsed. Apparently they hoped I wouldn't notice their blackened fingernails and dirty wrists.

I sent them back: "Go wash up for dinner."

This time they came back clean—not because they were convinced it was necessary, but because they were hungry. They knew that if they wanted to eat, they would have to be clean first.

The girls, on the other hand, had been coloring that morning. They'd handled things like construction paper, markers, crayons, tape, and pencils. Except for a couple of stray marker stains, their hands looked very clean—especially when compared with those of their male counterparts. When I asked the girls to wash up, they were enthusiastic. They loved the process—the sweet-smelling soap, the warm water, and the soft towel in the pretty bathroom.

The contrast is clear. Anyone could see that the boys needed to wash up, but they did it only because it was a means to an end. The girls weren't visibly dirty, but they loved the cleaning process and were willing to wash because they enjoyed cleanliness. They would have washed up *without* dinner.

Dinner is usually an opportunity for fellowship. God wants me to come clean before I enter fellowship with Him. When I want to spend time with Him, I need to make sure there's nothing in the way of our relationship. Just as the dirt on the boys' hands would have made it difficult for them to taste anything else, the sin in my life will taint the taste of my fellowship with God.

Washing up is like coming clean before Him. "If we confess

our sins, he is faithful and just and will forgive us our sins and purify us from all unrighteousness" (1 John 1:9). Now there's some good news. All we have to do is come to Him and admit we're dirty and that we don't want to be. He does the rest!

He wants "clean hands and a pure heart" (Psalm 24:4). He alone can make us clean and pure. No matter where we've been or what we've done, Christ's blood on the cross can pay our debt of death for our sins. That blood washes away our guilt like a big bottle of antibacterial soap.

I want a relationship with God more than I can say. And He wants a relationship with me. So why do I resist washing up before dinner?

"Rachael, wash up."

"But Lord," I reply, "I haven't been playing out in the mud, not for a long time now. I have only been coloring."

"Come," He says. "You may not have been in the mud, but you've wanted to be. And I can see some germs that you can't see. Let Me help you wash up—so that we can fellowship together."

A Moment of Introspection

- If you're a parent, how well do your kids wash up for dinner? How many times do they have to go back before their hands are clean?
- How would you characterize your fellowship with God? Why?
- What "mud" or "germs" do you need to let Him help you remove? When and how will you do that?

48

"It's your choice."

I was one of those children—the kind who has to touch the wet paint, taste the vanilla, and peek at the Christmas gifts. When I faced lousy consequences, they were often ones I had weighed and chosen.

I remember one instance in particular. My mom had been ironing.

"Don't touch the iron."

You probably already know where this is going. It wasn't the first time I'd been told those words. I knew the iron was hot, but wanted to touch it and see how hot it was. When mom left the room, I tested her wisdom.

The iron was *very* hot—blistering hot, in fact. For the record, it cured me of touching any other hot things. My mom and grandmother cried as I sobbed at the pain. They, too, were hurt by my bad choice. Despite their instruction, I'd chosen to do things my way.

Our choices, as members of the human race, began in the garden. Way back then Adam and Eve were given two options. Bottom line: self or God, life or death.

Eve chose what looked like independence and understanding, but was really death. It's easy to be critical of her decision all these years later. But the fact is that we're faced with the same choice daily—and we express the same tragic preference.

Moses, speaking before God's people were to go into the Promised Land, challenged the Israelites to choose. "This day I call heaven and earth as witnesses against you that I have set before you life and death, blessings and curses. Now choose life, so that you and your children may live . . ." (Deuteronomy 30:19). The same kind of choice is ours. It seems obvious, like trying to pick between chocolate and poison; but we regularly choose the poison and blame the effects of our choice on Him.

We must, as Joshua encouraged the Israelites to do, "choose . . . this day whom you will serve" (Joshua 24:15). It's impossible to sit on the fence and not make a choice. Not choosing is a choice; neutrality is not an option.

Jesus said, "No one can serve two masters" (Matthew 6:24). We can't choose to serve ourselves and God. It just doesn't work that way.

Rewards or penalties—those are the choices. Setting up consequences and carrying them out was a full-time job for my parents. I can only appreciate all their hard work now.

Children need to learn early that they have choices. They can choose to obey and enjoy the rewards of a long life on this earth that will go well with them. Or they can choose to disobey and reap the penalties.

The most difficult part of being a parent is watching kids make poor choices and having to live with the consequences.

One of the most rewarding parts of parenthood, meanwhile, is seeing them make tough, right choices and enjoying the rewards.

It's our job to set up consequences in order to train our children. Like a computer program, this involves a bunch of "if/then" loops: If you do this, then that happens. Clearly stated rewards and penalties ensure that all parties can know and weigh the options.

Like our children, we face choices. We don't have to choose God. We can choose ourselves. The consequences are clear.

His will is that all would choose Him. But not all will. He didn't make us robots; He gave us a choice.

A Moment of Introspection

- If you're a parent, what are some choices your children are facing?
- What choices have they made that were painful to watch?
- What penalties and rewards do your kids expect? What consequences do you expect to result from the choices you've made lately?

49

"Don't panic."

D o you know the number one emergency rule?
It's "Do not panic; remain calm."

I can't tell you how much we've used that rule at our house.

To little kids, everything from a splinter to an ant to a large dog to a beautiful sunrise can cause a moment of excitement that looks like panic. They don't know when a situation is really an emergency. If it's unlike anything they've experienced—and their experience is limited—they tend to panic.

Our little Elizabeth can panic over the sight of blood. In the summer at our house, there can be a bunch of blood flowing. Lately, if even a pale pink appears on her skin, Elizabeth is sure a Band-Aid, gauze, and tape are in order.

"I'm bleeding!" she screams. We're trying to teach her to relax and let us take a look. We clean the area and see whether medical attention—or just a kiss—will do the trick.

When panic sets in, objectivity bolts. It's almost impossible to think clearly when panic has been allowed to invade. When mental clarity is gone, confusion takes its place. In a panicked state, people faint, hyperventilate, "flip out," and behave in other strange ways.

That's why the first emergency rule is so important.

I had a chance to see this in action when Davis and the boys were out of the country on a week-long missions trip. They'd been gone for four days, and I was exhausted. Savannah Anne was the oldest one I had and, as helpful as she was, there was only so much she could do.

I sent the four kids out to play while I took a break to make pickles. (How crazy does that sound? I was desperate.) Little Ben was napping; I was chatting on the phone with a friend when it happened.

The recipe called for sliced onions. I was trying out a new kitchen gadget I'd purchased at one of those home parties. I hadn't seen it demonstrated, but thought I could figure it out myself.

"This thing works great!" I told my friend on the phone. It worked so great that I sliced off part of my hand along with the onions.

The pain was immediate, as was the blood. "Kim, I just sliced my hand," I told my friend.

"Are you okay?" she asked. "Do you need me to come over?"

"No, I don't think so," I said.

I think this is the part where I consciously didn't panic.

Unfortunately, I don't always follow that emergency rule. In fact, it doesn't always take something as serious as slicing my hand to get me to panic. No, I've been known to panic simply because things don't go the way I think they should. If I can't see how plans can work out, I panic. If others aren't cooperating, I panic. Instead of pausing and taking a deep breath, I let out a silent scream. I'm too sophisticated to scream audibly, but God hears.

And what about those bigger issues—unemployment, divorce, house fire, medical diagnosis, car accident, unplanned pregnancy, secret sin revealed? Any of these could elicit a panic response. Yet our heavenly Father gently encourages, "Don't panic. Stay calm. Take a deep breath."

He is there when the lightning strikes and the thunder rolls. When the waves are crashing and the rain is pouring down, He hasn't left. In all the commotion He offers His perfect peace that transcends all understanding.

He gives peace instead of panic, when only panic seems to makes sense.

A Moment of Introspection

- If you're a parent, when do your kids tend to panic?
- Describe a situation in your life that makes you want to cry. Have you allowed yourself to release the tension with tears? Why or why not?
- How could remembering that God is there bring you peace this week?

50

> **"Take out
> the trash."**

I must confess that I didn't hear this one much growing up. No, taking out the trash was my brother Rowdy's job.

But I do remember that *he* didn't like to do it much. And who can blame him? Yuck, what a job.

As I grew older, I realized that my brother and my dad weren't always going to be there to take out my trash. Bummer!

Eventually it was up to me. In college I got into a pretty good take-out-the-garbage habit. I may even have been a bit obsessive about it, since I hated the smell. I got used to taking out the trash, but I can't say I ever really liked it.

Then I met Davis. Before we got married, we went to premarital counseling. The counselor told us about the impact of expectations in a marriage. He gave us a list of things that had to be done in a marriage and a family. We were supposed to go through the list and mark who we expected to do the various tasks—wife or husband. There it was: "Take out the trash." I quickly marked *husband.*

Davis has been in charge of the trash at our house for most of our marriage, though there are times when I have to do it myself. Now, with the boys getting older, they can take out the trash. But it's not their favorite chore.

As a large family, we create a lot of trash—way more than the dumpster can handle. We also overflow the recycling bin. Sometimes trash day is embarrassing. *Did we really use all that stuff?* I wonder. *What must the neighbors think?*

Yet we have to take it to the curb for the city to pick up.

In the same way, we must also take out the spiritual "trash" that piles up in our lives.

I'd love to deny it, but I've got trash like that. I try to keep it hidden. Sometimes I ignore it, hoping it will go away. But I think those closest to me can smell it.

Sometimes I try to take it out secretly. I make a midnight run when no one is watching and put it in someone else's dumpster. *Who will know?* I think.

God does, of course. He wants me to take out the trash in my life. He even wants to *help* me take it out. That should be reason to celebrate! I don't have to get rid of all my junk by myself!

The rub comes when He wants me to get rid of stuff He calls trash that I kind of like. The definition war begins.

So what is this spiritual trash? It's anything that piles up in our lives, that smells, that we're not benefiting from—anything that clutters up our path to Him.

There's a list of "trash" attitudes in Ephesians 4:31. It includes bitterness, rage, anger, brawling, slander, and malice.

When we allow this kind of trash to accumulate in our lives, our prayers become a stench instead of a fragrant offering. Trash like this can lead to physical disease and personal disaster.

Our society has taken to ignoring, accepting, and dressing up this kind of trash. We've become trash tolerant, adopting a "Don't ask me about my trash and I won't ask you about yours" mentality.

That doesn't mean, of course, that God wants me to come to your house or heart and demand that you get rid of your garbage. But we're supposed to be available to help and encourage each other—even though we're responsible for our respective piles.

When confronted about our trash, we get defensive. "Who do you think you are to call my stuff trash?" we say. "You don't think you have any? I could haul mine out in one trip; yours would take all day!"

We can call trash whatever we want, but it's still trash. God wants it to go to the curb without delay.

The good news is that every day is trash day, spiritually speaking. Whenever we're ready, God is there to take it off our hands and replace it with His gift of grace.

Taking out the trash never sounded so good!

A Moment of Introspection

- If you're a parent, do your children have the same definitions of trash that you do? Why or why not?
- What are some things that clutter your path, keeping you from getting closer to God? Which of them would be hardest to get rid of?
- What would be the benefits to you if you cleaned up your trash? How can you start today?

51

> **"Are you
> ready yet?"**

Our four oldest kids take music lessons. Loading up the instruments and heading off for instruction has been part of our routine for eight years; days and times have changed, but we've consistently gone to lessons weekly.

After doing this for so long, we find this process can run like a well-oiled machine—or at least a well-oiled machine with some sibling friction mixed in to keep me on my toes, depending on God.

One morning, however, was an exception.

The kids were busy with a variety of responsibilities: getting Joseph dressed, brushing hair and teeth, making beds, straightening up rooms, packing lunches and snacks, preparing the diaper bag, getting together lists and coupons for "after lessons" errands.

For my part, Benjamin needed to be nursed, changed, and fed breakfast before being dressed and strapped into his car seat. All of us were taking care of the ever-important task of gathering instruments and music. Finally there was the vital goal of getting all of us and our stuff neatly packed into the van—a big job!

Even with all that organization, there's rarely a morning when I don't have to go back in the house for something: directions, coupons, a list, sunglasses. On this particular morning I needed a pair of earrings. I dashed into the house, leaving everyone else in the running car, thinking I was the only one not strapped in.

As it turned out, I'd missed something far more important than earrings. I found Anderson sitting at his desk in our homeschool room, examining one of the many creatures he'd found and brought home. He was thoroughly entranced in critter watching.

"Whoa, Anderson!" I said, not quite believing what I was seeing. "Are you ready yet?"

No, he wasn't. He was still in his pajamas.

At some point he'd stopped getting ready. He'd gotten up and gotten started, but had stalled out. He seemed to be in a fog, oblivious to the fact that the rest of us had been feverishly getting ready all morning long.

When I shocked him out of his creature study, he was embarrassed. He'd known all he'd needed to do. He'd been given time to prepare for the day. But he hadn't taken advantage of that time or the encouragement he'd received.

I discovered later that I wasn't ready, either. Oh, I was all dressed up and looked the part. Unlike Anderson, I didn't sport pajamas, disheveled hair, or unbrushed teeth. But I wasn't ready. I hadn't taken advantage of the time God had given me to prepare for whatever the day held.

I had my lists and coupons, my lipstick, and now my earrings. I had my purse and my water. But I hadn't spent time with God that morning, time when He could prepare me for what He knew I would face that day. I didn't seek Him and wait on Him in the early hours of the morning.

"Are you ready yet?" I could hear Him ask my heart. No, I acknowledged, I wasn't.

It's important to be ready for an average day here on earth. But it's even more crucial to be ready for the day of Christ's return.

I know how to get ready for a soccer game or biology class, but how do I get ready for Judgment Day? How do I get my children ready?

It's not as difficult as you might think. It begins by admitting my sinful condition, for which the penalty is death. This leads to my realizing that I need a Savior and the acceptance of Jesus Christ as that Savior. As the perfect sacrifice, He paid my debt by dying in my place on a cross because of His love for me. He came back to life, defeating death, offering me the opportunity to escape eternal separation from Him in hell by merely answering His call on my life to be His child.

Getting ready for the big day—the biggest day any of us will ever get ready for, a day far more important than any birthday or wedding or anniversary because of its endless impact—starts with me saying, "Yes, I believe. I know I'm a sinner who needs a Savior. I believe Jesus is that perfect Savior; I accept His gift of eternal life and want a relationship with Him."

He loves you. He died for you. He longs for a relationship with you.

He's coming back. Are you ready?

A Moment of Introspection

- If you're a parent, when was the last time your kids weren't ready for something? How could you help them to be ready next time?
- Are you ready for whatever life might bring your way in the next 12 hours? How could spending time with God help you to prepare?
- Are you ready for Christ's return? If not, what do you need to do?

"Get busy."

Each year we take a trip to the beach with my parents, Grannan and Paw. Having made the journey together for 13 years, we all look forward to it. We play Chicken Foot (a domino game), go crabbing, make sand castles, find seashells, play in the waves, swim at the pool, and stay up late with popcorn and movies. It's a blast!

But getting ready to go is a mammoth task. There's laundry to do. Floors need to be swept, mopped, and vacuumed so that no varmints move in while we're gone. And that doesn't include all the packing. All of this has to wait until the day before departure, or I have to start the list over.

A couple of years ago I started making lists for the kids so they could help me pack. They gather the things on the list; I check the items as I put them in the suitcase. It works well when we're all focused.

I will admit, though, that I spend a great deal of Packing Day saying, "Get busy."

There's so much to do that it's easy to get overwhelmed and distracted. I know from experience.

I was packing the girls' things. Savannah Anne had laid out their light pink cardigans, but Molly's was missing. I knew that if I didn't get it now I'd forget it—and Molly might catch a chill at night while we were crabbing.

So I left the suitcase and went into the laundry room to dig out the misplaced sweater. But on the way I noticed that the LEGOs were not yet picked up, the lunch had been left out, and the towels still needed to be folded.

Where were my little worker bees? I set out to find them. (It won't shock you to learn that I never got that cardigan in the suitcase, will it?)

I found them humming, but not to my tune. They were playing upstairs, as if there were nothing else to do.

I could feel the frustration building in my veins. I could feel a sermonette coming on. I could feel the need to restrain myself.

"Guys, what are you doing?" I asked. "What are we trying to get done today? Where are we planning to be tomorrow?"

The questions were rhetorical, of course.

"You have got to get busy!" I declared. "Work now and play later!"

The kids went downstairs and got to work packing and cleaning. Now that we were all back on track, it didn't take too much time. And after all, what would a vacation be if you remembered everything?

Like my kids, I too often have busied myself with the unimportant. My schedule is packed; I don't know whether I'm coming or going. I run after this and that, but nothing of eternal significance.

How busy should I be? Where's the line between relaxing and wasting time? When is it okay to just flip through a magazine? What does it mean to "get busy" for God?

Getting busy for Him is different from getting busy for me. Getting busy for me is exhausting, overwhelming, never-ending. Getting busy for Him is exhilarating, energizing, everlasting.

Getting busy for me is selfish. Getting busy for Him is selfless.

Getting busy for me means a full calendar with lots of things to do, people to meet, places to go. Getting busy for Him means a calendar that has room for the appointments He has for me— the neighbor who needs dinner, the girl at the checkout who needs an encouraging word, the friend who needs to meet for lunch and prayer, the mom who needs to get out of the house and meet at the park.

Getting busy for me ultimately points to myself, my talents, my accomplishments. Getting busy for Him points to His glory, His goodness, His faithfulness, His love.

God wants me to get busy. I can imagine He looks down sometimes and sees me totally distracted by the world and its frivolity and vanity, and shakes His head.

There's so much to do, so many really important things. There are people to encourage, souls to save, prayers to pray, orphans to love, truth to teach, captives to free, help to give, hope to offer, joy to spread.

It's time to get busy!

A Moment of Introspection

- If you're a parent, when and why do you find your-self saying, "Get busy"?
- Are you busy for God's kingdom, or just busy?
- According to the King James Version of the Bible, Jesus said He had to be about His Father's "business" (Luke 2:49). What do you think He meant? What part of "God's business" could you conduct this week?

BECOMING A CHILD OF GOD

This is the part of the book that I really wish I could sit down and talk with you about, face-to-face.

I would love to talk with you personally about this God I've come to know so well—my heavenly Father, your heavenly Father. I'd love to tell you about all the times He's shown me His love, grace, faithfulness, and peace. I wish you could hear my voice and see my eyes.

Becoming a child of God is not complicated or difficult. It starts with an acknowledgment of your sinful state, admitting you can't live a perfect life that would earn entrance to heaven. No matter how many good things you do, how much you give away, or how many people you help, you can't pay the price for your sins.

Yet they have to be paid for. The price is death.

But here's the good part. Jesus Christ has willingly paid that price for you. He was perfect, and therefore His death for your sins is acceptable. It cancels your debt! All you have to do is stop trying to earn your inheritance through your own acts, and accept His life and sacrifice as your payment!

Admit your need for God's forgiveness. This takes faith, but He provides that, too. Faith allows you to trust Him with all the details.

The good news just goes on and on. Not only did God create you; not only does He love you; not only did He send His

Son to die on the cross to pay the penalty for your sins; but Jesus also rose from the dead, conquering death! Not only did He claim victory over death for Himself, but He extends that victory to you when you accept His sacrifice on your behalf. A new life—can it get any better?

As a matter of fact, it can. Jesus, after rising from the dead, returned to heaven to prepare a place for you. Just for you! Imagine having your special place in His eternal kingdom.

I like to think mine has a wraparound porch with a beautiful garden. I'll be eternally serving tea while butterflies, hummingbirds, and stingless bees flit and buzz about. Perhaps it will always be warm on my porch, with a slight breeze. I hope you'll drop by for a visit and a cup of tea. We can talk about His faithfulness and wondrous grace. Oh, the joy we'll share—someday.

In the meantime, Christ has sent us a Helper. When you accept Christ's sacrifice and make Him Lord of your life, His Spirit—the Holy Spirit—comes to live in your heart. He guides you, comforts you, and teaches you. He even helps you pray.

Can you fathom it? The Creator of the universe sent His Son, Jesus Christ, to die for you. He raised Jesus from the dead, and together they're preparing a special, eternal place for you. While we wait for Jesus to return, the Holy Spirit guides us.

In Christ you're an heir to the Kingdom, one of God's adopted children. The Holy Spirit is a down payment toward your complete inheritance.

Are you ready to claim that inheritance? By His grace, you can take the step of faith and experience this new life in Him as you continue to walk by faith.

FOCUS ON THE FAMILY®

Welcome to the Family

Whether you purchased this book, borrowed it, or received it as a gift, we're glad you're reading it. It's just one of the many helpful, encouraging, and biblically based resources produced by Focus on the Family® for people in all stages of life.

Focus began in 1977 with the vision of one man, Dr. James Dobson, a licensed psychologist and author of numerous best-selling books on marriage, parenting, and family. Alarmed by the societal, political, and economic pressures that were threatening the existence of the American family, Dr. Dobson founded Focus on the Family with one employee and a once-a-week radio broadcast aired on 36 stations.

Now an international organization reaching millions of people daily, Focus on the Family is dedicated to preserving values and strengthening and encouraging families through the life-changing message of Jesus Christ.

Focus on the Family MAGAZINES

These faith-building, character-developing publications address the interests, issues, concerns, and challenges faced by every member of your family from preschool through the senior years.

FOCUS ON THE FAMILY CITIZEN®
U.S. news issues

FOCUS ON THE FAMILY CLUBHOUSE JR.™
Ages 4 to 8

FOCUS ON THE FAMILY CLUBHOUSE®
Ages 8 to 12

BREAKAWAY®
Teen guys

BRIO®
Teen girls
12 to 15

BRIO & BEYOND®
Teen girls 16 to 19

PLUGGED IN®
Reviews movies, music, TV

For More INFORMATION

 ONLINE:
Log on to
FocusOnTheFamily.com
In Canada, log on to
FocusOnTheFamily.ca

 PHONE:
Call toll-free:
800-A-FAMILY
(232-6459)
In Canada, call toll-free: 800-661-9800

Rev. 6/08

Encouraging
Resources for Parents

Being a Kid Can Be Dangerous

As the teenage years approach, many parents feel overwhelmed by the possible problems facing their kids: premarital sex, drug use, eating disorders, and pornography, to name a few. The *Parents Guide to the Top 10 Dangers Teens Face* will help you recognize a developing problem and teach you how to combat it. Previously released as *Steering Them Straight*. (Paperback)

Take Advantage of the Moments

Everyday experiences present unique opportunities to teach our children about God. But too often, we're not prepared to take advantage of those times — and the moment's gone. The *Power of Teachable Moments* shows us how to make God real to our children right now. (Paperback)

Parenting at High Speed

In the midst of today's frantic pace, you may find it hard to effectively connect with your kids. *Parenting at the Speed of Life* gives you 60 ingenious tips to use the ordinary moments of the day to capture your kids' hearts — without having to gather supplies, plan activities, or set aside big chunks of time. (Paperback.)

Printed in the United States
137646LV00001BA/2/P